Judgement Days
In a Mountaineering Life

By Tom Richardson

With a foreword by Andy Cave

Tom Richardson

First published in Great Britain in 2012 by

High Peak Books
7 Bradwell Head Road
Hope Valley
S33 9HD

Barry Fletcher
highpeakbooks@btinternet.com

Printed and bound in Great Britain by
CPI Antony Rowe, Chippenham, Wiltshire

ISBN 978-0-9532342-1-9 (Paperback edition)
ISBN 978-0-9532342-2-6 (Hardback edition)

Decisions made above the clouds aren't always
black and white

To Janet with love

Foreword

This wonderful memoir, packed with wry observation, sharp wit and in a self-deprecating manner leads the reader feeling how did one man do so much in just one lifetime and lead an expedition to Everest?

I first met Tom 25 years ago when I moved to Sheffield. He was warm, open and welcoming. Though an ambitious climber, he was a great team player and a true lover of wilderness. Much of his passion came from sharing his own knowledge and joy of mountains and crags; as he explains, to guide others is 'a great gift and an honour'.

In 1987, I made my first pilgrimage to the Himalayas, joining Tom and others to attempt the first ascent of Tupopdon, a 6,000 metre peak at the head of the Hunza Valley, Pakistan. Low-key, light-weight with an emphasis on fun and adventure, it was a perfect introduction and pointed to what could be achieved on a shoestring budget.

A year later, I'd been on four major expeditions and had been head guide on two commercial expeditions. Returning from an attempt on the southwest ridge of Annapurna III, I called in on Tom. He had bought a huge house on Stead Road, Nether Edge, with his wife just as I was leaving. Now I learned he was single, but the owner of the house.

"Where are you staying?"

"Nowhere" I said. To save rent it was customary not to keep a room while on an expedition.

"You want to stay here?"

I rolled out my sleeping bag and stayed for four years. Keen to know how we were doing as much as what we had done, Tom was a great mentor. They were glorious years and the characters that joined on the journey were many and colourful. As a landlord, he was extremely tolerant, welcoming waifs and strays, and, in his own words, Stead Road became an "unofficial, open invitation, international climbers' doss house." All this while Tom pursued a career as a management consultant.

Foreword

A new era began when Tom met Janet, the two of them sharing a love of nature, challenge and zest for life. When Janet's career offered exciting opportunities in the Third World, they couldn't resist; "We went for it. Sometimes you just have to." A decade of being based on and off in Pakistan, Bangladesh and China meant there were many more adventures and friendships in the Himalayas.

Trying to capture such a full and rich life in words is not easy, but Tom has excelled in a marvellous understated tone. This story is full of big climbing characters and Tom is candid about the loss that mountains can bring. . Ultimately though, for me, Tom's message is 'to go for it', and, crucially, to cherish the bonds that are forged along the way.

Andy Cave
Author & Mountaineer

Contents

Contents

Introduction

My aim in writing this book is to reflect on decisions and judgements I have made in the mountains and to try to draw some conclusions about them and their sometimes life and death outcomes. Good outcomes can be achieved despite bad decisions and sometimes vice versa.

I attempt to explore where the narrow line between adventure and misadventure lies and what place luck has in events. These are the stories of my own mountaineering experiences in the Himalaya and Karakoram over more than thirty years which I also hope are of themselves both entertaining and engaging.

Clearly the ability to make correct judgements is not simply the result of cumulative experiences; otherwise it might follow that the most experienced mountaineers would not die in the mountains. In reality judgement is impacted by many things including personality, other people, perceived expectations and the value put on the hoped-for outcomes.

The book does not aim to draw a glib or simplistic conclusion about the nature of such decisions, it is a personal story and others will arrive at different conclusions by different routes. Perhaps it raises more questions along the way about how we can survive the life-enhancing lure of adventure in high mountains. That is the nature of adventure itself.

My intention has been to write an account that is accessible to both mountaineers and non-mountaineers alike. I have attempted to keep the technical language and the detailed description of the climbing to a minimum, but where I have found it to be essential for clarity or brevity I hope it is still accessible.

List of photographs

Colour photographs   pages 127-134 (inc)

Black and white photographs

List of sketch maps

Judgement Days
In a Mountaineering Life

Chapter 1

On the Buachaille

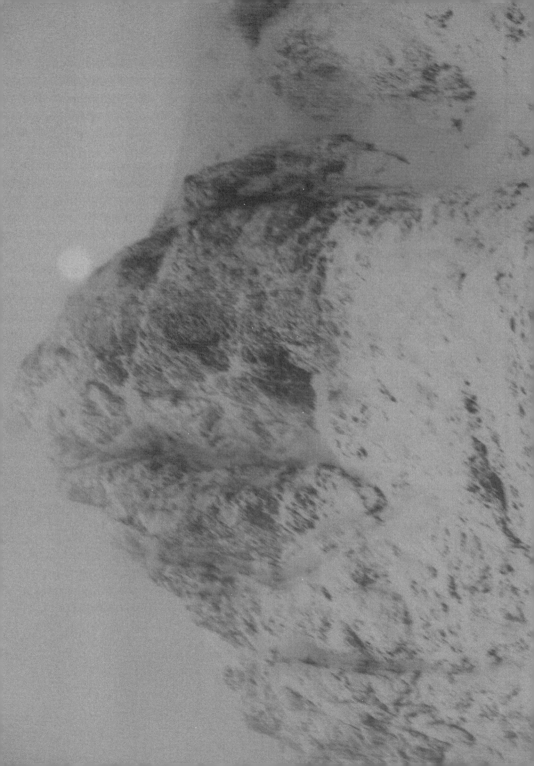

As I approached the familiar outline of the peaks of Glencoe on that January morning in 2009 I felt both a tingle of excitement at the prospect of once again being amongst such magnificent mountains and a pang of apprehension. There was snow cover down to road level and clouds hung languidly over the summit of the first and perhaps greatest peak in the Glen, Buachaille Etive Mor, often familiarly referred to by climbers as just "The Buachaille".

The Scottish Avalanche Service had rated the risk level as 3 on a scale of 1 to 5. Care and judgement would be needed. I was on my own for the day too, planning to climb with my friend James Thacker on the following day and then drive over to the east to do some interviews for Climb magazine (one of my several employers) after that. I parked the car just beyond The Buachaille and with slight reluctance stepped out of the warm, music-enwrapped car interior into the cold windy reality of the Glen. What to do?

Taking a popular, well-used trail, sticking to ridges wherever possible, seemed to be the safest option. I walked back up the road to the beginning of the footpath onto The Buachaille; it is a small track that leads to a former croft called Lagangarbh, now owned by the Scottish Mountaineering Club and often the foreground to dramatic photographs and postcards of the mountain.

Several cars were parked on the edge of the track and people were standing about tying boots and adjusting gear prior to setting off on walks or climbs. Amongst them by chance was Neil, a friend and client of KE Adventure Travel, another of my employers, whom I had led on a trip to climb Lhakpa Ri, a 7000m peak in Tibet. He had also signed up to come with me on a winter trip to Toubkal, the highest peak in the Atlas Mountains in Morocco, in a month's time.

On The Buachaille

It was good to see him again and meet his friends. I paused to chat for a while and then continued down the track and over the small bridge that leads past Lagangarbh and up the burn to its source in Coire na Tulaich, the usual walker's route up Buchaille Etive Mor. I was pleased to see that there were many footprints in the snow leading all the way into the gully formed by the burn. They disappeared out of sight round a corner and up the hill. I tried to work it out and guessed that about a dozen people were some distance ahead of me, out of sight.

From the head of Coire na Tulaich a relatively straightforward ridge leads to the main, north-east summit of the mountain, called Stob Dearg (1022m). I thought I'd just tag along.

It was great to be moving in the mountains again having spent much of the previous day in the car and I soon caught up with the first two people ahead of me. We exchanged greetings and commented how the weather was looking promising. There were blue patches of sky appearing between the clouds down the glen. I took some photographs and continued onwards.

At about three-quarters height I caught up with the trail breakers at the front of the whole group. We exchanged pleasantries and discussed the snow conditions. Certainly they were not perfect. The only exit from the coire was following the route of the normal footpath. The rest of the valley was either steep crags or currently overhung with cornices. One of the group asked me if I had been here before. I said I had but only in descent, after having climbed a few of the winter routes and summer scrambles on the north-east face.

I moved past them and started to break the trail in the ankle deep snow, heading towards the only cornice-free exit, which was also the path line. I crossed the gully to the left-hand side to avoid being directly under any of the cornices and slowly began working my way up the steepening snowpack. It was by then between shin- and knee-deep and I moved up using my ice axe as a third leg. I looked back down from time to time. The others were, I thought, wisely holding back just in case I slipped or the slope went. If either happened I calculated that I would probably just slide down the slope below. There is a steep drop down which the burn falls as a waterfall or forms as an icicle but it was a long way below and off to one side, or so I thought.

I took the last two or three metres very carefully. I made deep secure footsteps to help the others and used my axe as I stepped up. Finally I was at the top of the ridge. I looked across its flat top. The wind hit my face and I could plunge my axe into horizontal snow. I gently made a last footstep and began to step up.

The next thing I knew was that I was moving. Everything dropped away under my feet and as I glanced across trying to comprehend what was happening, I could see the nearby cornice curling over like a wave and dropping into the gap that had been created. I called out "avalanche", as much to confirm it to myself as anyone else.

At first I thought I could jump out of the way, but everything was by then moving. Almost immediately I was horizontal and going down. Amazingly the slide was relatively slow but the snow was solid and I can clearly recall my sequence of thoughts as I went down. In wet snow there is not the tossing and tumbling that can occur in powder snow in the Alps for example, it's more like a spill of wet concrete.

At first, well I suppose actually second, I was really disappointed and angry. I didn't want to die. I had a lot more life I wanted to live and even in that moment I already missed Janet, my wife. I felt bad for causing her inevitable grief. Of course my first conviction was that it was the end and that I, like so many other friends, would die in the mountains. As in a car accident when your entire life is supposed to flash before you in a second or two, all the foregoing flashed before me then.

Strangely, I wasn't overwhelmed with fear. It seemed to be a cerebral rather than emotional reaction for some reason. At the next moment I remember thinking that I should try to free my trapped leg that was bent back behind and under me somehow and also prepare myself by being as fully on the top of the snow pack as I could be. I should also have my ice axe handy just in case I got away with it. I hauled on my leg but it was stuck. I tried to sit up and after a fashion did. My axe was rather pathetically held in both hands across my chest in the position used to make a self arrest if you slip on a snow slope. Go down fighting at least, I thought.

Then, quite suddenly, it stopped. I had dropped a long way and the snow at the top of the avalanche had overlapped the snow lower down but come to rest about 10 metres from the drop down which the burn flowed. A proportion of the avalanche had poured down over the drop.

I dug my leg out and stood up. Uphill I could see a number of people standing up and brushing themselves down. Just a few yards away the two people whom I had first passed on the walk up were digging themselves out too; one seemed to have hurt his shoulder. Possibly we had got away with it and had a lucky escape? I called up to the others to see if they were alright and that everyone was accounted for. They said they were, but after a few seconds of looking added that people were missing. My heart sank. I took a few steps towards the gully and immediately saw a foot poking out from a heap of snow at the bottom. I called out.

Immediately the others started to descend to begin

digging out their friend. I got my mobile phone out to summon some help. Unfortunately there was no signal as the walls of the coire made an effective shield. I had to get down and out of the coire to call for aid.

As the adrenaline abated, shock began to hit me. God knows what it must have been like for the others still up there in the snow with their injured or dead friends. At the base of the gully I finally got a signal and called 999. I had some trouble making the call. My hands and voice were trembling with cold and shock and I had some pain in my leg. I wanted to return back up the hill and help with the others, but I was told to descend back to where my friends had parked their car and assist the Rescue Team from there. I reluctantly hobbled down whilst the others began an ordeal of several hours high on the mountain.

By the time I reached the car parking area, the Glencoe Police had arrived and the Rescue Team was on its way. I gave a statement to the Police and went over what had happened with the Rescue Team before they headed up the hill with avalanche probes and shovels. They were all fantastic people with a great passion for the mountains and a great desire to help others.
Some time later a helicopter from HMS Gannet in Prestwick arrived.

As time went on, it seemed less and less likely to me that anyone could have survived under the airless mass of wet snow, but the searchers continued and eventually the helicopter pilot very skilfully made several lifts from the gully to Fort William hospital. The team members remained hopeful and optimistic and told me stories of how sometimes people had survived and been revived in hospital after long periods buried in the snow.

The next to arrive were the press. One of their number was already with us, on a special assignment flying in the helicopter filming rescues for some TV programme or other.

It felt very strange being amongst the two groups of people attending the same event but with quite different objectives, one group trying to help and another trying to get a story. Initially I didn't speak to them and just sat in the Rescue Team's vehicle listening for any hopeful signs from the radio.

Eventually one of them asked me about where I was from and we talked about Sheffield and it's attraction for climbers. The conversation drifted into one about my late neighbour Paul Nunn (one-time president of the British Mountaineering Council, killed descending from Haramosh 2 in Pakistan in 1995) whom he claimed to have known along with other people whom it seemed were mutual acquaintances in the climbing scene. He said he used to be with the Rescue Team too. Eventually he asked me if I could say a few words on film for his local news for the record. He seemed like a straightforward chap so I agreed. This was another misjudgement. Whether he was genuinely trying to trick me or that the decision to publish the interview was not his I will never know. What I do know is that the next day many of the UK national and local papers featured it on the front page and it was sent all around the world on BBC News. Many friends across Britain and even as far away as Nepal were in contact about it and at home we were hassled by various news organisations for many days. It was the last thing I wanted to happen and I hope I never have occasion to put the lesson learned into practise. The lesson is not to trust news media people.

I called Janet. The timing was unfortunate to say the least. She was on the bus with her Aunt, her Mum's sister, going to visit the cemetery on the anniversary of her Mum's death.

As the afternoon wore on the rest of the group and the Rescue Team descended. It eventually became clear that three people who had been buried but taken to Fort William hospital, John and Eamonn Murphy from Northern Ireland and Brian

Murray from Tayside, had died. They were all members of the An Teallach Mountaineering Club. Their family and friends with whom they had been staying gathered outside Lagangarbh.

A sense of emptiness and loss descended around us. It felt like there was nothing more I could do. The Rescue Team prepared to head back home, and having told the Police where I intended to stay that night, I walked back to my car and immediately realised that I needed to be back home with Janet. I phoned James Thacker and cancelled our next day's plans, called in to the Police Station to inform them that I was going home, bought four cans of Redbull, filled the car with petrol and headed south.

I had flashbacks and nightmares about that day for a long time. I still do, but it is less and you just get more used to living with some things. In a way I don't want to not have them. I don't want to forget. Of course my experiences are much less painful than for those who lost loved ones, friends or family that day.

One frightening thing about the whole episode is the realisation that maybe if we had all made different judgements, nobody would have been killed. But it wasn't as if we didn't try, we had all convinced ourselves that everything was okay, or at least that it was okay enough, otherwise we wouldn't have been there.

I reflected a lot about this. All such judgements are about weighing up the likelihood of things that are marginal. In the past, had the decisions that had gone well really been more to do with luck, just disguised as good judgement, or had some of the many times when I had backed off a climb been overcautious and resulted in lost opportunities? How might any of us have acted without the reassuring interpretation of the Scottish Avalanche Service rating or the confidence gained by seeing other people out there taking away some of our doubts? It struck me my ability to make sound judgements in the mountains was an important part of my own identity, and that was now all called to question.

Thirteen months later, on 24th February 2010, my friend, fellow member of the Alpine Club and ex-colleague from KE Adventure Travel, Chris Walker was working as an instructor up on the Buachaille. In the KE days he had led trips to some high peaks in Nepal and in Tibet. He was strong, keen and had an infectious enthusiasm. In recent years he had also progressed to become a qualified mountaineering instructor working for various companies in the Highlands every winter. I hadn't seen him for a while but occasionally heard reports of how he was doing from mutual friends. He had reached the Stob Dearg summit with two clients via a route called Curved Ridge. The conditions were not perfect and on the descent, having looked down Coire na Tulaich and undoubtedly been aware of what happened to me the previous year, he elected not to descend that way but stick to the safer ridge line out of the way of obvious avalanche risk.

Chris and his client were both swept to their death from the ridge in shallow snow conditions a little lower down and were tumbled 500 metres all the way to the base of the mountain, looked on by their friends only a few feet away.

Chapter 2

An invitation that changed my life

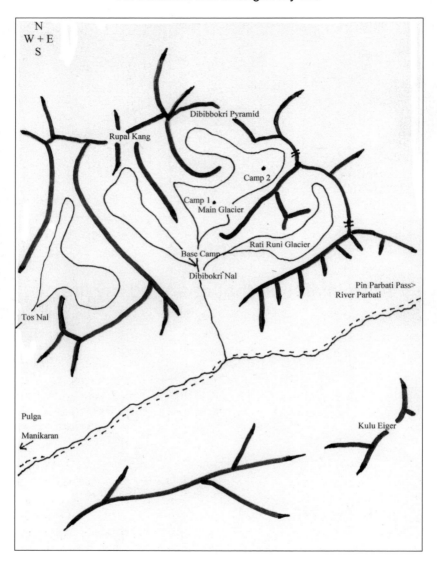

**Map of the Dibibokri Basin, Brent Himalayan Expedition
1979**

A few months over thirty years earlier I was sitting in a pub in the Peak District National Park which was a popular climber's haunt. It was, and still is, called the Moon and is in the village of Stoney Middleton on the edge of the limestone country that characterises the southern area of the Peak.

On the bar was a picture of Pete Boardman, the young climber who had reached the summit of Everest via the South-West Face on Chris Bonington's Expedition in 1975. He was posing on the summit and the caption read: "The nearest I've ever been to the Moon". To me it was like having Royal Approval that Pete had a few beers in the place at some time. I had attended an Alpine Mountaineering course in Switzerland run at the ISM (International School of Mountaineering) a couple of years earlier. Pete was the Director of the ISM and as it turned out also the guide, driver, cook and pretty much everything else.

Despite the grand name, he and a cupboard of assorted climbing gear were all there was of the International School of Mountaineering! I had all my own gear, but chose to use an axe that Pete said had been used by none other than Clint Eastwood during the filming of the movie of the book *The Eiger Sanction* in which the ISM had played a key role. He probably said that about all the kit in the cupboard to all his clients, but I believed it.

I learned a lot in that week even though I had previously climbed in the Alps and on Mount Kenya. Pete was the only person I had ever met at that time who had climbed in the Himalaya. Although very open, warm and friendly, he was a hero, more like a god. He was on a completely different level from bumbling amateurs like me.

Anyway, on this particular evening I wasn't really thinking about Pete. I was too busy chatting up my new girlfriend Alison and drinking far too much beer. Towards the end of a boozy evening, two friends, Rod and Sue Pawsey, who had been drinking and chatting with another group on the other side of the bar, strolled over. As always, without much ado, they got to the point and out of the blue asked me if I wanted to come with them and another friend Dave Hailey on a two-and-a-half month expedition to the Himalaya the following spring (1979).

They explained that two other friends they had met in the Alps that summer had been to a part of India called Himachal Pradesh, in the Kulu area, near a town called Manali. They had recommended that Rod and Sue attempt either a mountain called The Dibibokri Pyramid (6408m) or Rubal Kang (6150m). I had no idea what they were talking about and didn't understand anything they said after the word India.

They explained that there were no maps of the area but that when they parted company with these friends in the Alps one of them had made a sketch map on a beer mat or scrap of paper clearly showing "The Mountains". We would apparently have no problems finding them! Without a moment's hesitation, or the need to find out any more, I grinned and slurred, "Yes, definitely, of course, I'm in." From that moment, my life changed forever.

We spent the next few months persuading our employers to let us go, the Indian Government to allow us to come and various equipment manufacturers to assist us with the gear we needed to do it.

The responses were surprising. My employer, the Management Services Directorate of the London Borough of Lambeth, was under pressure from Central Government to cut its budgets and was pleased to be rid of me for a few months. Rod worked for an American bank, Sue for the NHS and Dave for Kodak. They all, for their own reasons, agreed.

We didn't hear from the authorities in India at that time, but decided to continue with our preparations on the basis that no news was good news.

Perhaps the most surprising of all was the generosity of UK gear companies who offered us a great deal of help even though our Himalayan mountaineering CVs were blank and the knowledge base of our powers of persuasion was nil. Both Gore-Tex and Hollofil were launched in the UK at about that time, so there may have been an element of being guinea pigs for these revolutionary new materials. Just as well they both did the job.

The peaks we were aiming for were over 20,000 feet, which in today's money is over 6000m. We knew it would be cold and so all invested in a pair of (heavy) Galibier high altitude double leather boots, the only type available at that time. Pete Boardman played a part once more, but again in his absence. In his gripping account of the ascent of the west wall of Changabang (also in India and called The Shining Mountain) with Joe Tasker, he described how they had home-made nylon overboot/gaiters that increased the warmth of the leather boots and kept them dry but still left the rubber sole of the boot free for climbing on rock. We had no aspiration (or ability) to climb anything as steep and scary as Changabang, but we copied the idea and Sue ran up a few sets on her home sewing machine. We secured them to the boots by stapling them with an industrial staple gun around the welt. They worked fine.

Eventually we were fully equipped and ready to go. A combination of new- and high-tech and old and home-made gear, arms full of jabs, four return air tickets to Delhi and loads of anxious anticipation and we were off.

Although expedition travel had become much easier than even twenty years earlier, when long sea or road journeys to faraway countries added to the tedium at the time and the rich adventure in the story telling afterwards, there was still quite a bit of tedium.

From Delhi we travelled by bus to Chandigarh, India's Milton Keynes, and then on in a dramatically overcrowded bus through the even more dramatic and sometimes scary mountain roads to the town of Manali. These journeys are so long you can't do them justice by measuring them in hours or days; perceived whole lifetimes slipping away seems like a better unit. I remember my friend, poet Kathleen Jamie vividly describing the catatonic state that she reached whilst travelling across Tibet, the state of mind that you reach when you've thought the last thought that you can think of and fantasised the last fantasy. Numb, but not numb in the places you would like to be.

Eventually we arrived in Manali. In the early 1970s it was

a popular stopping off point on the hippy trail. Unfortunately, not long before we arrived it had experienced one of its, at that time, not uncommon fires and most of the centre of the town had been burnt down. The setting amid pine forests and snow-capped peaks was beautiful, although the appearance of the town was obviously not. Nonetheless it was very appealing just to be able to get off the bus.

Today Manali is a rather different place. As the political situation in Kashmir deteriorated, urban middle class Indian newly-weds tended to find the romance of a house boat on the lake in Kashmir less attractive for their honeymoon than a new hotel in Manali. There are probably just as many hippies as there were 35 years ago, although hopefully not the same ones, but they now make up a smaller percentage of the transient population of the town.

On the precious scrap of paper in Rod's trouser pocket, along with the sketch map of "The Mountains", was also a name: a contact, a Mr Fix It who would be able to help us with all the arrangements to get us to base camp and back. The name was Tara Chand. We didn't have an address.

"Oh, just ask anyone, everyone knows Tara Chand," was the guidance we had received from the authors of the scrap of paper.

On the afternoon of the second anxious day of trying to track him down, we discovered him by accident sitting at the next table to us in a tea shop. He was a sophisticated and articulate local chap who was working on a German Government-funded project preserving the local Hindu Temples. Apparently he had been married and divorced three times and perhaps as a result many people seemed to be his relatives, although not all the children we met seemed to know that. He also did a bit of trekking and climbing and at weekends in the spring went skiing in the valleys towards the Rothang La. To access the slopes he used the road that for a few months of each year links the Kulu with Ladakh, the Tibet-like region of India to the north.

Beyond knowing that the region experienced a monsoon in the summer and was colder in the winter, we knew nothing of the local conditions. It was early April, too early as it turned out and it would take nearly a week before any mules were available to carry our loads. They were still all much lower down the valley in the winter pastures. We just had to hang out for a while.

Finally, by 17th April we were able to depart. Initially we had to take a local bus down to the village of Bhuntar where we would buy our remaining supplies from the market and cross the bridge to access the valley of the Parbati River, which flowed from the north-east. Our mountains were at the head of a tributary of the Parbati, the Dibibokri Nal, which flows south-east into the Parvati. We could drive to the holy temples and springs at Manakaran and use mules and then porters for a trek to our so called Turn Off Camp at the confluence of the rivers.

The bridge over the river was in its very last days of service. It was about a bullock-and-a-half wide and so could not take motor vehicles even in the days when it might have been strong enough. As a result the only vehicles that were on the other side had been driven, hauled and dragged across the river when the water level was at its lowest. Judging by the state of the bus on the other side, the last time that occurred was a very long time ago.

The road from the bridge at Bhuntar to Manakaran snaked its way high above the gorge of the Parbati River, with a big drop into the river on the right-hand side and steep cliffs and wooded hills on the left. At every bend on the road the

32

bus would turn but the roof seemed unwilling to follow. A gap of several inches would appear along the length of the bus, pouring sunlight on us and the other apparently unconcerned passengers, and then close jaw like as the turn was completed. By the time our expedition was over, this bus and the bridge would have been replaced by bright new ones. Probably just in time for both.

Manikaran is a small village based around a Hindu Temple that contains bathing pools from allegedly healing natural hot springs. It's a popular spot and when we were there it was rumoured that His Holiness, The Dalai Lama, no less, was coming for a visit to bathe in the waters.

At Manakaran Tara Chand departed, returning to attend to some other "family" business back in Manali, and left us with two young assistants, Likhtram and Merharchant, who would help us to reach Base Camp then return at the end of our trip to escort us back. They organised 8 mules and two muleteers for the next leg to the last settlement on the trek at a place called Pulga. Apparently after Pulga the trail was too difficult for mules.

After a rainy day spent recruiting fourteen porters in Pulga we set off in high spirits, excitement building, to begin the trek towards the Turn Off Camp. The porters carried their allocated loads, a few personal effects and (rather worryingly) between them had several very ancient looking rifles, apparently to do a bit of hunting on the return journey. The trail deteriorated quickly and soon we were clambering over rock-falls and edging along narrow tracks below steep cliffs before the valley opened out into beautiful high pastures surrounded by peaks.

Unfortunately our high spirits were short-lived. By the first evening the porters went on strike.

Looking back on it, they were probably justified too. They claimed that they had walked further than one day's worth and the river confluence, our Turn Off Camp, was further away than we claimed.

The late 1970s was a period of conflict and confrontation in the world of industrial relations in Britain. I know: I was working in the public sector in what is now rather chillingly called Human Resourcing, but then had the only slightly better term Personnel Management. I was also obviously not very good at it.

The porters claimed that it would take a further two days to reach Base Camp. We thought not. We had our trusty sketch map. They lived there. We called their bluff; they demanded more money; we called their bluff again. They picked up their rifles and (somewhat to our relief) went hunting. This was a tactical misjudgement on our part that we would have to live with for many weeks.

We spent the best part of a further week using up precious food and fuel shuttling all our loads up the valley to the Turn Off Camp. It was a dramatic spot at an altitude of 3770m, surrounded by snowy mountains and just downstream from a peak we nicknamed The Kulu Eiger. We subsequently learned that that was, for understandable reasons, its correct name. We spent several further days hauling everything up the gorge of the snow-covered Dibibokri river to the place which, for want of a better term, we declared to be Base Camp.

Base Camp was set amid some huge snow-covered boulders at a place called Rati Runi Thaitch. We were already struggling with the altitude, the exertion, the cold and our necessarily self-imposed light rations diet.

Our Base Camp kitchen, located under an inclined boulder, was comprised of two ancient but reliable half-pint, brass tanked, paraffin-fuelled Primus stoves, a stubby-handled pressure cooker and a couple of pots. The water supply was gathered in strategically placed pots and mugs under drips of daytime melting snow. It wasn't much, but we thought of it as home.

By the 5th of May we were ready to explore the mountains and set up an advanced camp in the side valley, on the Rati Runi Glacier, from where we would climb some easy peaks to acclimatise for the main event on the Dibibokri Pyramid (at the head of the accurately named Main Dibibokri Glacier).

We only had two tents, so struck Base Camp to carry them higher and make an advanced camp. Dave and I had a very early American version of the now popular dome tent design. It was super lightweight with an inner and flysheet and was supported by two crossed over fibreglass poles, but lacked any storage space. Rod and Sue had opted for a stormproof but heavier box-framed tent developed from Annapurna and Everest Expedition tents of the early part of the decade by the legendary mountaineer Don Whillans. The more snow that fell on it, the more stable it became. The two little tents, ours bright green, theirs red and blue, always stood out like welcoming beacons against the white and grey of the mountain landscape.

It snowed during the afternoon of our arrival and then the weather went into a night-time deep freeze. Ungloved fingers stuck to metal and breath turned to an icy veneer around the hoods of sleeping bags and across the inside of the inner tent.

We decided to attempt the easiest-looking peak in the valley, which we subsequently learned was at a height of 5735m. I was, as they say, psyched but wracked with anxiety about what lay ahead. Would I be up to it, would I cope with the altitude or would it be the end of my Himalayan dream? It nearly was, but not in the way I had anticipated.

Leaving many hours before daybreak, using the light from the chilled and fading batteries in our head torches and panting clouds of steamy breath into the cold dry air, we began to work our way up the easy lower slopes. The plan was to take an upward diagonal line to a col and then ascend the steepening ridge to the snowy summit. Moving unroped in knee-deep snow, we alternated the task of breaking trail. At one point I was a little bit ahead when there was a load bang and the slope began to crack into a slab avalanche. I turned to escape to safer ground, but at every step the crack lengthened many metres either side of me. With a surge of adrenalin I sprinted for safety, terrified and gasping for breath. Roped up together we would not have stood a chance. I thought about Nick Escourt, not that I ever met him. He was a regular expeditioner with Chris Bonington and had been swept away in an avalanche on an easy-angled slope on K2 the previous year. Doug Scott, on the other end of his rope, lived only because the rope broke.

We took a more direct line up towards to the col after that. Eventually we reached it and Rod and I broke trail to the summit, plodding through the snow and scrambling over the odd rock step. The view from the summit was fantastic. It was what I had come for. In one direction the Parbati South peaks, including the Kulu Eiger, all covered in snow and just catching the early morning light looked, I later wrote privately in my diary, like a fairy castle. In the other direction we could just see the pointed summits of Rubal Kang, Parbati (North) Group and the Dibibokri Pyramid. I was on my first Himalayan summit and I was very pleased.

The only slight disappointment was the cairn. So we weren't the first, but what the hell?

We made a rapid and direct descent to cross the lower slopes before the sun made them even more dangerous and we were back at camp by 9.30am.

Fortunately it snowed big wet flakes all that afternoon, so further climbing of the steeper peaks in the area was out of the question. We descended to re-establish Base Camp and address the main challenge ahead.

The next few days were depressing. Several more feet of snow fell, most of them pinning us in our tents at Base Camp. On some days Dave, my tent companion, silent with his book much of the time, would only leave the tent two or three times a day to relieve himself and return with the same conclusion. "Well, I can't see us doing much tomorrow," he would philosophise.

After snowfall a good but scary spectator sport was to watch the avalanches pouring down over the surrounding cliffs off the neighbouring peaks.

Eventually, despite the conditions we decided to start to plough our way up the Main Glacier to establish a camp or two below our objectives. There was a tension between us now, born of tiredness, altitude and anxiety. Sometimes it slipped out, but mostly everybody held it inside. Four people together but somehow alone. On the first foray up the Glacier, after about four hours of trail breaking in deep snow under what became a blazing sky, we dumped our loads on a mound of snow-covered moraine. We were exhausted and fractious with each other. Sue, still acclimatising, threw up.

Back at Base Camp, the evening brought thunder and lightning all around us, but little snow fell. For the next few days a period of clear, stable weather continued and we were able to return in half the time to establish an Advanced Camp at our gear dump and push on up the snow-covered moraine below the ice fall from an adjoining glacier, poetically called No. 2 Glacier. Somewhere safely in the middle of it all there was a large boulder set in a wide flat area in the snow. We declared it to be the next camp site and, like real mountaineers, called it

Camp 1. And what a camp!

Looking downhill in the direction from which we had come, you could see the peaks on the other side of the Parbati valley. Behind us the Dibibokri Pyramid soared upwards and to one side the Main Glacier continued to sweep down from a col on the south side of the Dibibokri Pyramid. We later learned that it may have been called Homes Col. Ascent from that col seemed the most, or rather only possible route.

Although short on food, one thing that we did have in a plentiful supply was medications of various sorts. Normally none of us were keen on taking anything, even a modest aspirin. We'd been taking anti malarias since before our arrival in India, although it seemed rather an unlikely thing to be struck down with at this stage. Again, having gleaned the information from Pete Boardman's book, we took something called Ronicol Slow Release which was in theory supposed to dilate the blood vessels and reduce the likelihood of frostbite. It might have in theory, but as I later found out in practice it didn't. We also took occasional non- barbiturate sleeping pills. Another mistake, as it turns out that sleeping pills suppress breathing, which is the last thing you need suppressing at altitude. In fact, all of it except for perhaps the vitamin pills was in retrospect a complete waste of time.

Once the new camp was fully stocked, having again shuttled everything up the glacier we began to focus on getting up the mountain.   We reckoned that from our camp it would take about two hours to the base of the col. The plan was to make a camp on the col and climb the pinnacle ridge to the summit from there.

We decided to go for it, gathered the minimum gear, including only one tent (our little green one) for the four of us and set off. Within minutes of cresting the first rise I realised

38

that once again we had underestimated the scale of the country. I could see clearly even in the half-light of the pre-dawn that ahead lay an ocean of snow- covered crevasses and moraine.

After about four hours we stopped for a discussion about what to do. It was 7.30 in the morning. We were still a long way from the bottom of the col, let alone on top of it. Sue and Dave in particular were struggling with the altitude and the knee-deep snow. The period of good weather appeared to be changing too. Red-tinged cirrus clouds had been replaced by a lower series of similarly coloured ones clinging around the highest peaks. If we had another multi-day patch of bad weather we had little chance of getting up anything. More seriously it would be a grim prospect indeed to be stranded, four in a tiny tent in a storm high on the ridge.

Without much confidence in the likelihood of summit success, but full of adrenaline, I persuaded the others that we could shed even more of our gear and go super light and make an attempt on the mountain while we could. We could give it a shot and get as far as we could.

On reflection this seems to illustrate the poor quality of decision making that happens in groups. My ego and drive didn't really allow the better judgements of others to prevail.

The route to the col was in four parts: a level section to the base; a short, steeper snow slope and then a longer, easier-angled snow slope that led to a rocky/shale section just below the col.

By now the sun was on the slope. The conditions were pretty bad. With every step up a slab of about a metre wide and several inches deep would break off and the footstep had to be made in the soft snow underneath. It was undoubtedly very dangerous terrain with a high risk of triggering a slab avalanche.

Rod took over the trail breaking at half height. It was exhausting and scary. We all knew what the conditions meant. I later wrote in my diary:

"To be perfectly honest, although I was aware of the conditions, I was also summit bound."

I was going well and Rod, Dave and I took turns to break trail. As well as it being the wrong time of day, we should also have chosen a route which didn't go straight up the snow slope: we didn't.

Approximately 50 metres from the top, just below the rock/shale section and safety we again heard and felt the vibration from a loud bang; it was like the shot from a gun. For a second we all froze and then turned and descended as fast as we could. We had triggered the whole snow slope to break and crack across its surface, but by some miracle the top slab had not separated and avalanched down. If it had released and started to move there was little doubt that we would all have been buried for ever under tons of snow here in the middle of nowhere.

As soon as we all had reached safety at the base of the slope I burst into tears. I had been so geared up and suddenly it was over, but fortunately we were not. We were safe and unhurt.

I cried uncontrollably for a time and then spent several hours apologising for embarrassing everyone (although it was me who was embarrassed). I surprised myself that I cared so much about getting up this mountain, although I suspect that the stress of events so far accentuated it all.

It seemed that we had got away with it a second time. We returned to the gear dump and the four of us sat out a wild and windy night in one tent. We called it Camp 2.

As predicted the weather did break and we remained tent-bound by the storm the following day.

When the weather cleared next Rod, Sue and I returned to Camp 1 to collect the remaining gear (including the second tent) to make Camp 2 a bit more manageable. Cumulative exhaustion was getting to Dave so he stayed at Camp 2. Rod (unusually for him) struggled back from Camp 1 to Camp 2 fully half an hour after Sue and me in the full fury of an afternoon blizzard, heroically carrying the sloshing half-full jerry can of paraffin, without which we would not be able to melt snow and keep hydrated. We were all exhausted and getting more so.

On the next break in the weather, Rod, Sue and I headed back up to the col. This time we took a line on the far left side of the snow slope following a slight rib. The snow conditions were much better and we were on the slope much earlier in the day before the sun reached it. I gained the top first, climbing the last bit of frozen shale on the front points of my crampons and driving in the pick of my ice axe above my head. I was staggered by the fantastic view. It was bitterly cold but it was great to be there, if not alone then at least on my own in this wondrous place. I waited for Rod and Sue to arrive but they stopped below the steep shale section. I took some photographs, very conscious that this might the high point of the trip, then I watched Rod and Sue set off down and, resisting the temptation to continue on a bit along the ridge, descended after them.

I later wrote in my diary that, "I was excited and filled with joy as I sitting glissaded down the lower slope to catch up with Rod and Sue, confident that at least we could give the mountain a go."

Back at Camp 2 Dave was feeling better and seeing us

descending had started to make brews for our arrival. He said he regretted not coming with us.

The 24th May was yet another cold and early start, but it was to be "The Attempt". It felt great that all four of us set off up our steps of the previous day. The weather looked fair and there had been a good night-time freeze. This time when I arrived at the col the others were right behind and together we marvelled at the fantastic views all around. We then struggled to put on harnesses and tie on to the rope. It was so cold it was nearly impossible to make fingers work to tie ropes or buckle straps. As before, I was keyed up and wanted to get moving.

Our plan was to turn left at the col and climb the steepening pinnacled ridge, hopefully to the summit . The first part, which was relatively easy angled, looked hard enough; near the top it looked very daunting, being mostly on steepening rock. Eventually we were ready and Dave and I set off over the first pinnacle or gendarme. It was quite awkward climbing in big boots, crampons and our bulky wind suits.

Rod and Sue watched my rather ungainly efforts from below and, as it turned out wisely, decided to explore the mountain on the other side of the col. Dave and I continued upwards. I led over two more tricky pinnacles and then up an easier snow slope. We were trying to move together roped up to increase our speed. The next pinnacle I turned on the left side and crossed a worrying snow-covered rock slab above a big drop and then went up a short, steep rock wall. I placed a rather poor piton, very aware of the difficulty of the climbing and how bad it would be to fall off the ridge. Finally I was on an easier section and although I didn't have a belay I pulled gently on the rope to bring Dave up. It wouldn't budge.

After what seemed like a long time I decided to descend a bit to see what had happened. I was getting very cold. I found

Dave nearly at the top of the rock pitch carrying coils of rope in his hand. Clearly the rope had jammed somewhere. Gasping for breath he also told me about how when he crossed the snow-covered slab, it had avalanched below him, which quite understandably scared him a lot. I didn't like to ask about how much slack rope he was carrying in his hand at the time. If he had fallen, we both almost certainly would have gone.

I led over a couple of easy snow mounds and was about to start the steepest section on the ridge so far when Dave announced from below that he couldn't go on. The altitude was too much for him. Initially I was shocked, but if he felt that he couldn't, then he couldn't. He knew best how he was. We would descend.

We paused for a few moments to take some photographs and absorb the view. Camp 2, far below, looked like two tiny brightly-coloured ladybirds on a huge sheet of white paper.
We began our descent with Dave going first and me behind. When we reached the notorious and now snow-free slab, we realised that we could not retrace our steps. Without the snow cover we could not cross it. After a bit of exploration we found a steep, loose gully leading down on the Camp 2 side of the ridge. I made a belay just below the top of the ridge and Dave descended with me giving him a rope from above. He down climbed about 30 metres before reaching a bank of snow that gave a route back to the ridge and the col. Below the snow bank there was a series of long drops towards the valley floor. Dave slithered the final few metres in the loose rock and snow before finally coming to rest.

It was then my turn to descend. It was vital to do everything right. Panting hard with fear and the altitude, I secured myself with a sling and arranged the rope to abseil down the gully. As I was abseiling on the rope double, I only reached about two-thirds of the way down. Concentrating hard I carefully secured myself again, tied one end of the rope to myself in case I dropped it and pulled the rope through the anchor above. All went well. I set up a second anchor on a big rock spike to make another abseil which would get me down to Dave. I abseiled carefully, stepping down gently, finding footholds in the loose rock with my crampons to avoid putting too much strain on the anchor and to avoid knocking stones down onto Dave who was huddled at the side of the gully below me. I reached the snow slope not far from him. What a relief!

After catching my breath and exchanging a few words, I pulled on the rope to retrieve it from the anchor, but this time it jammed solid. It just wouldn't move. So near to safety, I could have cried, but this time I was focused on getting down. I knew I had no alternative but to climb back up and free it. I tied on to one end of the rope in the vain hope that if it all went wrong something might hold me. I had to solo the steep, loose gully and if anything went wrong Dave could do little to help me. Breathless and frightened I arrived back at the abseil point. I secured myself again and unhooked the rope from the projection on which it had jammed below the anchor point.

I arranged the abseil again, untied myself and gently began to abseil down. About halfway down the block on which the rope was anchored and from which I had abseiled before suddenly gave way. I fell backwards through the air, off the cliff and hit the steep snow slope well below Dave. I tumbled down it initially head first on my back, but managed to turn round. My ice axe, attached with a sling on my wrist, was out of reach. The slope only had a light snow cover on it with rocks underneath. I started sliding fast towards the drop below. I clawed at the slope with my hands, my face, my feet, anything to try and stop. Eventually I did. Then a torrent of snow and rocks from above caught up and swept over me nearly setting me off over the lip, but I held on.

In my diary soon after the event I calculated that I must have fallen several hundred feet. Probably a wild exaggeration, but it was far enough. I stood up and brushed myself down. The only damage was a broken filter on my camera, lost sun glasses and a rip in my wind suit. Thank God for my helmet. I untangled the rope which had wrapped itself around my body and called up for Dave. I rather expected him to be sheltering from the onslaught at the base of the gully, but there was no sign of him. I couldn't understand it. Could he have been swept down from his perch by all the rocks that came down with me? Oh God! With no real purpose I summoned as much breath as possible and called out his name in a hoarse croak. There was no response.

Eventually, much to my relief, I saw him far below underneath the cliff I had struggled not to fall off. He had witnessed the whole thing and had thought that one of the large boulders that flew past him, down the slope and over the cliff was me. He had found a route round to the base and was desperately searching for me amongst the debris.

Despite all of this we soon regained the ridge lower down and then the col. Not long after, Rod and Sue returned from their reconnaissance of the other peak. They had seen the whole thing too and, after checking that I was okay (which, I was surprised myself, I seemed to be), expressed optimism about a possible route to the summit.

Later again in my diary I wrote that, "I knew I wasn't going to die when I fell." As I write this now I would say that it is a great illustration of both the power of self delusion and the fact that I didn't die, but doesn't prove that my optimistic mantra was right. On the other hand optimism in the face of contradictory evidence might be the ingredient that makes you claw the snow to slow and stop you before you go over the cliff. Without the fight I think I would have gone over.

An Invitation that Changed My Life

The next day Dave was still not feeling well, a combination of altitude and exhaustion. He had also, quite reasonably after witnessing the events of the day before, a sensible reluctance to do it all again, so he elected to stay at Camp 2.

So it was that Rod, Sue and I set off yet again up the interminable slopes to the col. Our footsteps of the previous day were obliterated by a night-time snowfall. This time I took the precaution of putting on my harness and tying a loop in the ends of the rope into which a karabiner could easily be clipped if need be, all before I left the relative warmth of the tent. We were going to have a go at their peak, the one to the right of the col.

From the col, the going was easy up a sinuous ridge to Rod and Sue's high point of the previous day. We paused in the clear early light to take some photographs and then continued up a steepening wall of snow and ice that led to the summit. We climbed unroped the whole way except for the top few metres when we used them for the final icy section.

To me it felt as if finally we were in the right mental state and the mountain was in the right condition for us to be able to climb it. After all the struggles, at last it was going okay. Or perhaps the power of self delusion made it seem like we could influence the physical world by our mental state.

As I pulled up onto the small summit, clouds rolled in, at first obliterating the view and then reducing visibility to just a few metres. I got a nose bleed that dribbled blood down my face and beard. We had made it, but only just and we were only about half-way. We took some photographs and started down. We still had to get all the way back home.

With the cloud and limited visibility came wind and swirling snowfall. Our footsteps had disappeared and route finding - particularly on the less steep terrain - became very challenging. In the whiteness, what looked like a snow slope would turn out to be a small cornice above a drop that would break away beneath our feet. It was all very frightening. Psyched and focused for so long, after the summit the plug had been pulled. I was nearing exhaustion and I began hallucinating. At one point, not far above the col, when the clouds cleared I saw a family of sea lions basking there. It didn't seem odd. I remarked upon it to Rod. He didn't comment. We carried on down.

Eventually the tents appeared, we staggered down and with much relief got in them. Dave supplied tea. We had made it. We had no idea whether it had been climbed or even exactly how high it was, although somewhere around the 6000m mark seemed likely. Between ourselves we called the mountain Kulu Ganesh, the Gate Keeper to the Kulu Valley.

It later turned out that during a snow-free period in September 1973, members of a team comprising Rob Collister, Geoff Cohen, John Cardy and Dick Isherwood succeeded in climbing the peak that had caused Dave and I so much trouble the previous day. They just referred to it as Pt 20101 and reported on it in the 1973-4 edition of Alpine Climbing, the then journal of the Alpine Climbing Group.

We never did find out about "our peak", contemporary maps of the area don't even show it as a peak separate from a larger summit of 6507m further south-east along the ridge, but in the end, it doesn't really matter either.

Inside my sleeping bag that night and for the first time for a long time I felt my body inside my layers of clothes. I didn't recognise myself. I and therefore all of us had lost a lot of weight.

Initially unable to move, following a rest of two days after summiting we began clearing the area. We carried everything down from Camp 2, collected what remained at Camp 1 and headed for Base Camp.

On arrival in Base Camp I pulled off my woollen Dachstein mitts which I had worn over thinner Damart liner gloves. The finger ends on the liner gloves had worn through many days before and I was shocked and frightened to see that several of my fingers were black with frostbite. I hadn't even noticed it coming on. My hands had been cold all day, but that was normal. Cold, tiredness, hunger, dehydration and poor equipment had all contributed. I had read horror stories about fingers and toes having to be chopped off after frostbite. I was scared. I didn't want to lose mine. For now all I could do though was let Sue bandage them up, try to keep them from getting infected and hope for the best.

Likhtram and Merharchant turned up at the Turn Off Camp at the appointed day but disappointingly without any porters. So, between the six of us, as we didn't have any food or fuel to carry, we transported everything in huge loads in a two-day walk back to Pulga. We spent the night as guests of two holy men in a remote temple in the forest. One was Indian, the other strangely a French Parisian who had very much gone local. Nettles were cut from the surrounding clearing and a delicate soup was made from it for us. It was a gentle blessing and a helpful transition back into the rest of the world.

On the remaining trek back to Manakaran the next day most of our thoughts were about food. We bantered with each other about how much curry we would eat in the first local eatery that we reached. These places are generally not of the highest hygiene standards, although freshly cooked vegetarian food eaten with clean, washed bare hands minimises the risks. In the event we did all put up a good performance consuming seconds and thirds and copious amounts of rice before sleeping for the last night nearby.

Next morning we boarded a brand new bus to Bhuntar. Within minutes Rod and Dave were violently ill. By that afternoon, all of us were being sick out of the bus window and having to stop the vehicle to get off, suffering from diarrhoea. Back in Manali I developed a large abscess from a small cut on my leg that oozed pus.

For five days we were all laid up sick in a tourist lodge in the town, unable to summon the strength to get the bus back to Delhi. It wasn't the ending we had hoped for. Boiled water and local yogurt were the only things we could consume.

Eventually our stomachs began to settle, the sore on my leg improved a bit and the black crusts on the ends of my fingers sloughed away revealing, much to my relief, bright new perfect pink finger ends underneath.

On the 13th of June we made it back to Delhi and finally flew back home to London on the 18th.

In the end, by the two most significant measures, the trip was a great success. Most importantly, we had all returned safely and also we had climbed two summits. Along the way we had made lots of decisions, which by some measures at least could be considered to have been right because they led to us achieving success. The reality was however that in many instances we succeeded despite the judgements we made rather than because of them.

We had arrived in India naive and ignorant and had been given a fantastic opportunity to learn from experience. It was a dangerous place to learn and we were lucky to get away with it.

For me at least there was the initial self delusion that

experience in the well-mapped and much frequented Alps and elsewhere had somehow equipped me for an unusually snowy spring in a remote corner of the Indian Himalaya. We had been low on knowledge and judgement as well as much else.

Dave never returned to the Himalaya and that summer married his girlfriend Christine and drifted away from our circle. Rod, Sue and I have remained good friends to this day.

For me, I was hooked, committed to a life of adventures in high mountains and, although a conventional life of home, work and girlfriend ran alongside, I remained on that course.

Chapter 3

Late for work

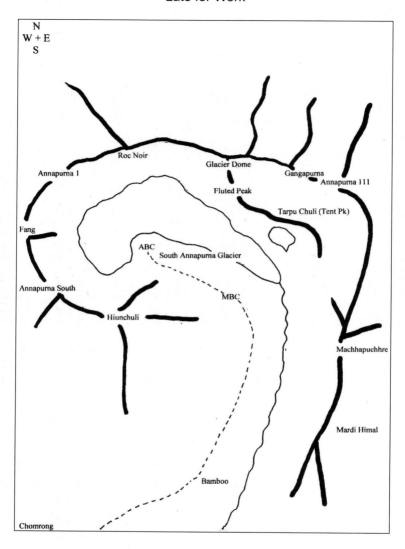

N
W + E
S

Roc Noir

Annapurna 1

Glacier Dome

Gangapurna
Annapurna 111

Fluted Peak

Tarpu Chuli (Tent Pk)

Fang

ABC
South Annapurna Glacier

Annapurna South

MBC

Hiunchuli

Machhapuchhre

Mardi Himal

Bamboo

Chomrong

Map of the Annapurna Sanctuary Area of Nepal

"I'll kill de bastards, kill dem, I swear it. Tomorrow, before dawn I'll get my gun and my Khukri knife, track dem down and kill dem – for sure, don't you worry," ranted Captain Gurung, the retired Ghurkha Officer and proprietor of The Captain's Lodge in Chomrong (a small settlement on the trail that leads to and from the Annapurna Sanctuary in Nepal).

We were pleased to have someone so obviously, even if rather overenthusiastically, on our side. We had first arrived in Chomrong at the end of the third day's trek towards to the Sanctuary, where we planned to climb Singu Chuli and Tharpu Chuli (otherwise known as Fluted Peak and Tent Peak), two of the satellites below the huge South Face of Annapurna 1.

The previous overnight point of the trek was a particularly welcome sight at the end of a long, humid, rainy and leech-infested day. We were soaked to the skin despite waterproof jackets and umbrellas and still had unstoppable trickles of blood from leech (known as jukah in Nepal) bites running down our skin and clothes.

In those days there was no road into the mountains from the main town of Pokhara and we had trekked from our hotel in the centre along the trail of the Mardi Khola Valley, through water filled paddy fields to the few buildings at Suilket. The next morning we had climbed up and past small farms growing millet in immaculate terraced fields. Millet is the prime ingredient in locally brewed alcohol.

The village of Dhampus marked the top of the ridge and the beginning of the rain forest. The muddy trail then winds in a green tunnel and eventually leads to the small settlement of Tolka in which we found Ram Lodge. It had been a demanding day that had begun at first light with the daily sorting of all our gear and supplies into porter and animal loads. We were tired and had only just begun the expedition so it felt great to be in the dry, to have a good meal of the local dhal bhat curry prepared by Dawa, our cook, and to get into our sleeping bags.

Ram Lodge was a small, unassuming building on two floors under a corrugated metal roof. We (friends Richard Haszko, Martin Whitaker and I), slept upstairs in the open space that took up the whole of the floor. Half of our expedition kit was stored with us. Downstairs Phurba Tamang, our Sirdar (or foreman of the porters and other local staff), and the rest of the porters and the cook team slept alongside the remaining gear.

That night the rain of the day turned into a violent storm with thunder and lightning. It was the late monsoon of September 1985. It was an early miscalculation. We had read Chris Bonington's account of his expedition to the South-West Face of Everest. His team had reached the summit on 24th September, so we thought that would be the time to go. Whilst

September is a good time to be above 8000m to avoid the jet streams, it is a bad time (as we found out) to both trek and climb at lower altitudes.

From our sleeping bags we could hear the rain pounding on the metal roof although we couldn't see anything because as well as it being dark outside, the glassless window frames were all secured closed with solid wooden shutters. At some point during the night one of the shutters was prized open from the outside and a person or several people entered the room under the cover of the sound of the pounding rain and crashing thunder.

We only noticed when we woke up that the window was damaged and several packs containing equipment, clothing and money were missing. The thieves had been well organised. They must have been watching us the previous day and had followed us. They knew exactly how to carry out their plan. Despite the conditions outside they had sorted through the bags of stolen items in a nearby terraced field, taking only things that they thought could attract a good resale price in the trekking equipment shops of Pokhara or even Kathmandu. Other items were left strewn about and the area was covered in footprints.

We were left without most of our money, mountaineering clothing and some gear, although fortunately we still had our boots and of course we had been in our sleeping bags when the robbery had taken place, so had those too.

It had taken us months to save up for, acquire from sponsors and even design some of the gear and now, after just two days on the trek it was gone. Disappointed, shocked and even a bit embarrassed, we thought that the chance of ever getting any of it back and therefore having any chance of climbing our mountains was, to say the least, extremely slight.

Phurba immediately organised a search and arranged for a couple of the Sherpas in the team to retrace our steps back to Pokhara. They would ask the locals on the way if they had seen anyone with our gear or been offered it for sale and, although it was a long shot, see if they could find the thieves themselves in Pokhara. They would report the incident to the Police in Naudanda village. We were not at all hopeful.

We decided to go for it anyway and next day to continue towards Annapurna Base Camp. We could at least trek there and maybe we might meet up with an expedition from whom we could borrow or beg some replacement gear. We would be hopeless at trying to track down the thieves ourselves, didn't have enough money to buy any replacements nor the time to get back to Kathmandu - a long day's bus journey from Pokhara and the only place where such purchases might realistically be possible.

We set off once more, somewhat depressed at the prospect. The next day's destination was Chomrong, about 6 hours' trek from Tolka, and it was still raining.

On our return to Chomrong at the end of the trip, when we first met Captain Gurung and told him our tale we were pleased with, if a bit worried by, his reaction to it so the following morning it was with a certain amount of relief that I noticed that both the man and his shotgun were still in place and that the Captain was nursing a "fever" that he assured us was not the result of the previous night's chang (the locally made alcohol).

As other people subsequently said, his reaction was probably more about the threat to the reputation of the area which would negatively affect his business, rather than exclusively concern for our misfortune. I like to think it was a bit of both.

From Chomrong the trail to the Sanctuary then re-enters

the forest. Today it is a well marked and trodden trail with excellent stone- and cement-built lodges that offer a wide range of food from a menu and even can arrange a hot shower. It is within the world famous Annapurna Conservation Area Project (ACAP).

In 1985 it was very different. The first overnight stay was at a place called Dovan. It was in a small structure made from split bamboo wattle with plastic sheeting on the roof and a wood fire burning in the low chimneyless interior. The next day, still in the green tunnel of the forest and flanked by the huge blank cliffs on either side of the Modi Khola (river) that leads down from the Sanctuary, we paused in a clearing under a large overhanging rock called Hinku Cave to take lunch. From here we got our first views of the magnificent mountain known by many as Fish Tail, whose real name is Machhapuchhare (6993m) rising 4000m directly above us.

Machhapuchhare is a holy mountain to local people. It has never officially been climbed to its summit. The only attempt was in 1957 by a British team led by Jimmy Roberts. Climbers Wilfred Noyce and David Cox climbed to within 50m of the top via the north ridge, but did not complete the ascent. They had promised not to set foot on the actual summit. Noyce said at the time that:

"It looked as if the Goddess had drawn her firm line here, at least for these two respectably married suitors."

Since then, the mountain has been declared sacred, and it is now forbidden to climbers. After their near ascent they moved on and made the first ascent of Singu Chuli, which at the time they called Fluted Peak (one of our objectives). Wilf Noyce was killed five years later with his partner in a slide on easy ground from Peak Garmo in the Pamirs. His partner was the then up-and-coming star of the next generation of British climbers, Robin Smith. Sobering thoughts.

The overnight stop was at another simple settlement at Bagar at the end of the forest, where in the morning the weather cleared to give our first and breathtaking views of Gangapurna and Annapurna 3 at the head of the valley. Our route would take us left past a place that is incorrectly called Machhapuchhre Base Camp to Annapurna Base Camp. A Base Camp for Machhapuchhre would at the very least be on the same side of the Modi Khola (river) as the mountain. Annapurna Base Camp (aka ABC) is also a misnomer as expeditions to the vast South Face are set up on the other side of the South Annapurna Glacier, on the same side as our objectives, Fluted and Tent Peaks.

In 1985 there had only been one successful ascent of Annapurna 1 from the Sanctuary. It was Chris Bonington's large-scale expedition that made a new route up the steep 4000m South Face and it made the summiteers Don Whillans and Dougal Haston, as well as Chris himself, household names in the UK. Nonetheless even in 1985 there were a couple of more solidly built trekker's huts at ABC with a welcome fire inside. The altitude is about 4000m, which is high enough to bring on at least pounding headaches and nausea for most people when they first arrive.

Once rested we set up our tents amid the boulders in the mist and blowing sleet. There were no views of either Annapurna 1 just looming above us or our own peaks to the north across the glacier. With the last of our money we paid off most of the porters and hoped and gambled that the message sent back with the Sherpas also reached our agent Mike Cheney in Kathmandu and he would send more with which to pay the porters for their return trek at the end.

We settled in to acclimatise to the altitude and for me recover from the cold and chest infection that had established itself annoyingly as the trek progressed.

I had first met Richard a few years earlier outside the Albert Premier mountain refuge in the French Alps. My girlfriend at the time Alison and I, along with two other friends were, as was customary with British climbers, bivouacking a short distance away from the hut rather than staying in it to save money. We recognised Richard's climbing partner, known as J.T., from the North London Mountaineering Club and it turned out that Richard was also a member. Confusingly he didn't live in North London, but Sheffield, on the edge of the Peak District National Park, arguably the heart of British rock climbing.

He told me that he had been a student in London but had returned to his home city where, despite being now in his 30s he had recently been back to college to complete a post graduate course in Human Resource Management. He said that as a result he was teaching related subjects in the local Further Education College. He also said that from where he lived it took just 15 minutes to drive to the nearest climbing area. It all sounded good. This brief conversation led not only to our lifelong friendship, but also when I returned home at the end of the holiday to hatching a plan for a major life change. I was certainly ready for one. My employer, Lambeth Council, was in a mess having been led by Councillors who were more intent on scoring political points against the government than delivering services. The Brixton Riots had partly taken place outside our flats and I was really fed up with spending weekends escaping from London. I wanted to escape altogether.

We sold the flat, bought a small house in Sheffield and I secured some work teaching most evenings and some afternoons at the local Further Education College. I also got a place on the same course that Richard had completed a couple of years earlier. I anticipated that I would be able to get round my afternoon absences from it to fulfil my teaching contract or manage to be in two places at the same time, which somehow I did!

It turned out that whilst I was juggling my time to do everything, the reality of Richard's teaching was somewhat less taxing than he had made it sound. Since finishing the course his entire work commitment was just one hour a week teaching. If I had known that back in the Alps I may not have hatched my plan in the first place.

Alison and I also decided to get married. We had been together for four years and living together for two of them. At the time it seemed like the most likely part of the plan to succeed, but in the event was the only part that didn't work out. After about six months looking for work in Sheffield, Alison got a job as a temporary secretary in a small steel company in Sheffield. Some months later she chose to have a different life and a relationship with her then boss.

Sheffield has long claimed to be the Climbers' Capital of the UK. It certainly was in the early 1980s. Others might describe it as being cliquey. Richard was a long-established member of the clique or community. As my personal life unravelled, I was immediately unconditionally and warmly welcomed into the wide circle of Sheffield-based climbers, male and female and of all ages. The key figures were inspirational people who all had a life-changing impact on me, including Al Rouse, Rab Carrington, Paul Nunn, Andy Pollitt, Jim Curran, Geoff Birtles, Geraldine Taylor, Steve Bancroft and, a year or so later, Joe Simpson and Andy Cave. It was during one of many regular evenings in the pub with Richard and several of these characters that we decided go to Nepal and try to climb Fluted and Tent Peak.

The daily weather pattern at Annapurna Base Camp was clear until about 9 am and then clouding in and deteriorating to snow and sleet by the afternoon. Usually it cleared again in the evening to give cold starlit night skies. I decided to rest for a couple of days to try to clear my chest infection. Richard, Martin and Phurba set off with Dawa the cook and some porters and set up a high camp on the other side of the South Annapurna Glacier below Tent Peak.

Over the next couple of days they hiked up the nearby snowy lump known as Rakshi Peak (named after the creator of commercial trekking in Nepal, Jimmy Roberts's dog), explored a possible route on Tent Peak and returned to Base Camp. From the top of Rakshi Peak they could see the features on Fluted Peak some distance away and Tent Peak close by.

Back at Base Camp Richard reported that neither of the possible routes up Fluted Peak looked very feasible. The glacier leading up to the attractive but steep West Face was very dangerously crevassed. Our heroes Alex MacIntyre and John Porter had gone this way in 1982, but they were a lot better than us. A few years later the accomplished alpinist Trevor Pilling and his partner would also disappear without trace somewhere amid these seracs and crevasses. The alternative ridge route would require some steep climbing up the fluted snow on the flank of Tent Peak and then a long committing traverse towards Fluted Peak. With either simple fear or fear disguised as rational good judgement we probably made the right decision and concentrated on getting up Tent Peak.

Down in Base Camp I had learned that a Japanese climber had been trying to climb the flutings on Tent Peak. He had failed fifteen times so far this season. Even the veteran British mountaineer Al Burgess (who had a commercial group in the area) had failed and had headed home.

The force of the arguments against an attempt, let alone a successful ascent, were piling up.

On the plus side an Irish Trekking group had very kindly loaned and given us a range of bits and pieces to replace some of the stolen ones, so given good weather it might make it possible to give the climbing a go.

Richard, Martin and Phurba decided to rest at Base Camp and as I was feeling somewhat recovered, I set off next morning to spend a night at the high camp and acclimatise. They would come back up the following afternoon. It would also be the highest night I had spent alone on a mountain.

The next morning, thirty minutes above our camp, I was surprised to come across another small tent. I t was that of the Japanese climber who was now on his sixteenth attempt to climb the flutings on Tent Peak. I then hiked up Rakshi Peak and enjoyed the magnificent views including Annapurna 1, Hiunchuli and across to Machhapuchhare. I agreed with Richard's analysis of the route to Fluted Peak.

The others arrived back at the High Camp in the early afternoon. The next morning we woke early. It was dark and the weather looked ominous. Clouds had moved in early. I t would be an all too easy and quick decision to just go down. The trouble was that we knew, as is always the case, that we would certainly regret it almost immediately and for a very long time after if we did. It was not entirely because we had come so far that we felt we should try, but more that it might be okay and we would never really know that unless we went up to check. We might still regret it, but we might, just might not. It is always difficult to find the line that divides trying enough from going too far.

We set off. It was still dark. The route initially traversed under the face of Tent Peak from north-west to south-east. At the time there were no guide books and little information about the area. These days the flutings taken by the Japanese climber are considered the Normal Route. The most likely route for us seemed to be a wide gully or couloir that joined the South-East

Ridge. The two problems about which we were not clear were: what was the ridge like between where the couloir joined it, and the summit. We knew there would be at least one additional difficulty on it and that was a large rock tower halfway along. Could we climb it, or climb round it somehow? In fact the entire route had been climbed before but we did not know that, so approached it with no knowledge and only our judgement to go on.

The couloir was excellent, providing more than 300 metres of steady climbing. We climbed unroped, enjoying cramponing up the frozen névé. Initially we took the right-hand side, then climbed through a narrow section and on to the left and then finally up a steep wide bowl that joined the ridge.

The way ahead to the summit didn't look very encouraging. The snow was softer under a slight crust giving a generally unconsolidated, scary feel. However on the left-hand side of the rock tower there was a narrow ledge. We roped up and moved along it, placing a rock peg for a belay. I led up a gully to just below the ridge. Phurba followed while I made myself into a human anchor and he soon moved past me and popped over the top. By the time we were all on the ridge together, an hour had passed and the clouds were closing in fast. Martin led off on our rope of four along the knife edge ridge towards the summit. It became increasingly difficult to distinguish between the clouds swirling all around and the white snow of the edge that we were carefully making our way along. If somebody had fallen or the ridge had collapsed on one side, I supposed we should have had to jump down the other side, but doing so is so counter-intuitive I doubt if it would have happened.

The summit was perfect, a small area where the South East and North West Ridges joined. Holes in the clouds opened to offer windows of magnificent scenery.

The effort and the altitude (5500m) were making my cough quite debilitating, but I was running on natural adrenaline. We took some photographs and headed down.

Any summit is always only halfway and the cloud and sunlight were softening the already treacherous snow. The visibility on the way back down the ridge to the rock tower was even worse. It was approaching white-out, a condition in which it is impossible to distinguish snow from cloud or where you are putting your feet. I could just make out a slight shadow on the snow of my own feet, but that was about all. The soft snow was also sloughing away down either side of the ridge. A fall from it would almost certainly take us all almost 500m down the Face.

Martin rigged up an abseil anchor on the rock tower by placing two pegs and Richard abseiled off over rocks to the top of the pitch I had climbed on the way up. We continued down the ridge to the point where the couloir met it. Thunder now boomed all around us and strangely it was hot in the clouds. We urgently needed to get off the mountain but were concerned about the safety of the now soft snow and loosened rocks in the couloir. Our helmets were also amongst the items stolen earlier in the trip. We had to do something and, in the absence of many options, I just set off down facing inwards, using the front points of my crampons and my axe in what the French call the *piolet ancre* position. Unavoidably we bombarded lumps of snow and ice down on each other as we hurried down to safety; fortunately there were no major strikes.

At the bottom the weather deteriorated further and the others hurried off back to camp. I followed more slowly, pausing in the cloud, dark and falling snow to clutch my chest, cough and feel sorry for myself.

Martin and Phurba decided to return to Base Camp and Richard and I decided to rest and enjoy one more night at this great location, or in other words were too tired to descend. It continued to snow all night and the following day we struggled over snow-covered rocks and steep grass back to Base Camp.

That night Dawa made a cake to celebrate the fact that we had climbed the mountain. It was nearly Richard's birthday and Mingma, one of the Sherpas, had arrived at Base Camp with some fantastic news. He had brought money from Mike Cheney in Kathmandu, letters from friends and family and the news that the robbers had been apprehended. They had been spotted by Mingma at the bus terminal in Pokhara and he had summoned the police.

Martin was still keen to try Fluted Peak, but for the rest of us it was time to go home.

Back in Pokhara we visited the Police Station where the robbers were being held to record the theft, collect anything that might have been salvaged and to see if we could get a report from them for an insurance claim. There was a small queue of locals ahead of us awaiting the attention of the Duty Officer. The two men in front of us were both in a heated state, arguing with each other about something in their local language. When their turn came, the Officer stood up and calmed the shouting before listening carefully to each man in turn. When they had presented their cases he picked up a large stick from behind his desk and started to set about one of them with it. Instant justice, I assumed.

As a result of this we were not particularly confident about a satisfactory outcome to our enquiries; in fact at that point not being beaten with a stick would have been good enough. Nonetheless we waited our turn and were soon summoned into the Police Chief's office. The Police Chief spent some time explaining to us what a great job his officers had done and what vermin the thieves were. He said he was happy to report that he had all our equipment and clothing (but strangely not the cash) for our collection. Unfortunately he could not just hand them over to us because he had the criminals in custody and there would be a court hearing in two days' time. We had to both wait and turn up at court.

On the day of the court hearing we attended the dingy building on the edge of town. The walls were bare and there was little furniture inside. Chickens clucked peacefully for scraps around the floor. The two suspects were presented to the judge in chains and handcuffs.

After an extensive deliberation in Nepali which we didn't understand, they were found guilty and sentenced to a staggering seven years in prison. When I got a translation I was shocked and appalled and a part of me deeply regretted the whole incident. Perhaps we should not have bothered to report the incident in the first place? In its simplest terms, we were relatively rich and they were poor. A prison sentence could only make things worse. I felt guilty and impotent to do anything.

There was however also a further obstacle to the return of our gear. The court could not release it without a signed affidavit from some legal person as the court could not take the Police's word that the gear was ours. The details of every item were therefore painstakingly recorded in triplicate by hand and dutifully sent off to someone to be signed.

The next day, with optimism fading, we went to collect our stuff from the Police station. The Police Chief was pleased to see us yet again but explained that in order to release our gear we must also pay 10% of its value to cover their expenses. Once again, despite the money from Mike Cheney, we were broke. As we finally got up to leave the office I asked the Chief about the harshness of the sentence of the two young thieves.

"Oh," he said with a casual wave of his arm, "that was all for show. We could not afford to keep people like that in prison. They'll be out next week and probably will be working as a porter for you on your next trek!"

I didn't know whether that was good or bad. A week later we flew back to the UK.

In those days there was no internet, international phone calls were difficult and expensive and post from Nepal, if it ever arrived would take weeks. My employer by now of just one year, Sheffield City Council, had expected me to return to my desk ten days earlier, but had heard nothing from me, so it was with some anxiety that I turned up besuited and with a detailed explanation/excuse prepared.

I expected at the very least to receive some sort of disciplinary warning. Instead I was greeted with the same warm, friendly smiles that had waved me goodbye all those weeks ago. The Assistant Director said he was pleased and relieved to see me as they had been putting off the promotion interviews for Principal Training Officer for ten days, but had been forced to hold them today. My interview was in fifteen minutes! I had forgotten that I had even applied for the job.

By the end of my first day back at work, far from having a warning on my record I had been judged the best candidate for promotion. It wouldn't work twice!

Chapter 4

A Legacy from Al Rouse

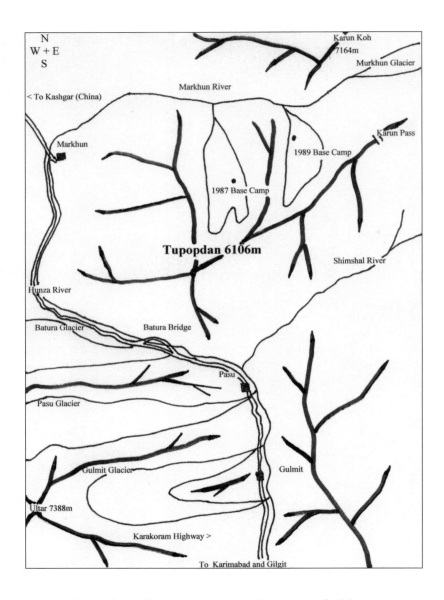

Map of the Tupopdan area, Northern Pakistan

Most weekends were spent climbing. On one occasion we were at Stanage Edge's High Neb Area with a team comprised of many of the big names in British climbing at the time plus me, including Al Rouse, Chris Bonington, Steve Bancroft and Geoff Birtles (the then Editor of *High* Magazine). One typical incident of that day was when I was leading Chris Bonington, no less, up a route called (strangely enough as it turned out) *The Blurter*. Al Rouse called up from below... "Tom, you're climbing really well these days." Momentarily I felt great. Steve Bancroft, 1970s gritstone climbing star, quickly chipped in from nowhere, "Well you must have been f***ing s**t before then". Hoots of laughter all round at my expense. The climbing scene had some robust banter.

From 1984 to 1985 I was a lodger, along with another climber friend Neil Foster, in Al Rouse's house. Al had also recently split up with his girlfriend but had managed to buy her out of the deal and keep the house. Al was in many ways at the centre of the Sheffield and UK climbing scene and indeed a major player in world climbing. He had made many bold first and solo ascents on both rock and ice around the globe. In the 70s he climbed a lot in the Alps and in South America with his friend Rab Carrington and more recently had been on several trips to the mountains of Asia, including several with Chris Bonington. He was it seemed to me to be on the brink of becoming, or in waiting to become, the next elder statesman of British climbing whenever Chris might decide to step down.

In addition to the three of us plus our girl friends, at weekends the small terraced house would be a base for a wide range of climbers. On one weekend we may have Chris Bonington and then the next Johnny Dawes. I was enjoying my job working for Sheffield City Council and also every evening after work, weather permitting, we would go climbing. There were no climbing walls, climbing was always outside. The choice of style was either what is now known as Trad (with a rope) or soloing. We did both. I would often change out of my work suit at the base of the crag, fold it carefully and shove it into my rucksack and hope it wasn't too crumpled by the morning, which it usually was. Al was a far better climber than me, well actually he was a far better climber than nearly everyone, but he was also an excellent coach and the sheer joy that climbing at any standard gave him was infectious. I not only got better because of Al's mentorship, but better than I could have previously dared to imagine.

On another Saturday morning Al and I drove out to the Winnats Pass in the Peak District. This steep-sided, narrow limestone gorge is a dramatic feature through which a minor road winds, giving one of the few throughroad routes between Sheffield and Manchester. For safety reasons climbing was not then permitted.

A Legacy from Al Rouse

However, throughout the spring several Sheffield based climbers quietly had been attempting to climb a route on the highest of the buttresses. One rival team to Al included a very strong young climber called Mark Miller who some might have said was a rising star in British climbing. Tragically, later in October 1992 he was killed in an air crash. Before his death, Mark with his friend Andy Broom set up an international mountain adventure company called Out There Trekking (OTT), who coincidentally many years after Mark's death would employ me on their team.

The only previous ascent on the face in the Winnats Pass had been made using artificial aids many years before and the rusty scars of some of the hammered-in ironmongery were still in place on the side of the vertical and otherwise smooth face. The rock presented a single pitch of climbing, but unfortunately it ran into near-vertical unclimbable grass at the top so once it finished the leader had to be lowered back down to the start. Al climbed the route brilliantly and I lowered him off from the top. It had taken a long time and, even standing below paying out the ropes it looked hard.

"Right," said Al, once back at the belay ledge," your turn." There was no escape and anyway someone had to take all the protection out. I struggled, grappled and pulled my way up. At the top I unclipped the anchor, Al took in the rope onto the second runner and I began to descend, half down-climbing, half being lowered off. I removed each of the runners as I reached them, hoping that each next one would hold my weight if I slipped. For its height the crag is probably the most exposed in the Peak District because it sits vertically above a steep grass slope of several hundred feet directly above the road. A loose rock tumbling down onto the traffic would have been bad enough, two climbers a lot worse. Today with modern sports climbing techniques the whole project would have been different and we would have been back down at the car much sooner, but our method worked.

Back in the nearby climbers' café in the village of Stoney Middleton, where the new routes record book was kept, Al judged that the route justified a grade of E2 and called it (whimsically, in the face of the climbing ban on the crag) *Rite of Way*. In a very gentlemanly if strictly inaccurate way he included my name in the first ascent. I, despite having no delusions about my real role in the ascent, was chuffed. Other climbing friends were not surprised that Al finally claimed the prize, but were amused that I was on the ticket too.

Climbers tend to be very particular about the details of claimed first ascents. Heated arguments frequently occur about the climb, the ethics employed and the correct grade. People who knew me understood the reality and took it, with typical humour, a stage further. It triggered a minor trend in which some people claimed I was involved in an important hard first ascent when I wasn't even present on the day! Today, after quite a few ascents, the route is graded much harder at E5 and access is still problematic!

In the summer of 1984 Al and Chris Bonington had attempted a mountain in the Karakoram of northern Pakistan called Karun Koh (7164m). They had not made the summit due to bad weather but had spotted some interesting unclimbed smaller peaks of about 6000m nearby. One of them it turned out was called Tupopdan. It would be a part of Al's huge legacy to climbing.

In August 1986 Al died, trapped in a storm whilst returning from the summit of K2 (the world's second highest peak) having made the first British and alpine-style ascent. He left an unfillable void in all our lives.

Although the most obvious thing to non-climbers is the

danger and risk to life involved, to most people the process of becoming consumed by a passion for climbing leads at the same time to a refusal to acknowledge the reality, or to live by some distorted self-delusion that it couldn't happen to you. Al was a great friend, a mentor and an inspiration to many people. He had got away with so many bold adventures that, although perhaps never conscious and certainly never expressed, we perhaps all hoped that he had solved the problem of how not to die in the mountains and that we might learn it from him by association. Al was not the first climber that I had known who had been killed, in fact over the previous few years many of his contemporaries had died pushing at the boundaries of what might be possible in the high mountains.

I had booked a place on a course at the ISM (International School of Mountaineering) in Switzerland in 1977. The then Director, Dougal Haston, who had climbed the Eiger Direct, the South Face of Annapurna and made the first British ascent of Everest via the South-West Face, died before I attended. His role was taken by Pete Boardman, who ran my course but then also died along with Joe Tasker on the unclimbed North-East Ridge of Everest in 1982. At that time British mountaineers were at the cutting edge of developments, but over a decade or so most of the best of them died pursuing the cause. Al, though, was both the closest person to me from that group to die and had the most influence on me up to that time. To most sane people the sensible reaction might be that having realised that you had lived a selfish life based on rigorously not acknowledging the reality of the risks, you might be both embarrassed and relieved to have got away with it and adopt a different way of life, but only a few climbers do.

There are, as far as I can see, at least two blocks to this otherwise sensible course of action. The first is that climbing, mountaineering and the love of mountains are all highly addictive. I imagine that, as with drugs, withdrawal from both the activity and the lifestyle requires time, determination and support. The second is the lack of realistic alternatives. Almost by definition, activities that are safer do not provide the life-enhancing experiences that climbing and mountaineering can provide. Sometimes chosen alternatives are just as dangerous as climbing. Our friend Ian Tattersall died paragliding in Greece, having given up mountaineering because he had a young family.

Al's loss left me feeling empty and much of my routine life seemed less appealing, less meaningful. On the other hand I didn't have much heart for heading off on another expedition to the big mountains either.

In early 1987, as I was recovering slightly from the initial shock and loss, a plan began to germinate. Richard, my friend and partner from the Tent Peak trip, mentioned the idea first. We could go and climb Tupopdan, the peak spotted by Al from Karun Koh. I was torn - both fired up with excitement and yet filled with doubts and fear.

A team was gradually assembled by Richard and at first it seemed both a disparate and an unlikely one. Joe Simpson was still recovering physically and psychologically from his epic misadventure in the Peruvian Andes (described in his much acclaimed book *Touching the Void*).I had first met Joe and his partner on the trip, Simon Yates, when they came round to our house to consult with Al about his experiences of climbing in Peru in general and about their climbing objective, Siula Grande, in particular. The few weeks that followed would change both of their lives, but Joe's in particular, forever.

Andy Cave was doing his "A" levels, having left school without any to follow his Dad's route into the now defunct coal mines of South Yorkshire. He had taken up climbing and discovered a natural talent for it whilst on strike to stop the pit closures.

John Stevenson had been a talented rock climber a decade or so earlier but had spent little time in the mountains and quite a bit in the bars and pool halls of Sheffield of late.

Steve Ralph (aka Jungle after the always lost navigator in the spoof mountaineering book The Ascent of Rum Doodle by W.E Bowman) and his friend Hugh Morley were tagging along as supporters, trekkers or climbers who might have a go if it was okay.

We must have looked more impressive on paper than we did in reality. Chris Bonington, having seen the mountain with Al, chipped in as the Patron of the venture. The Mount Everest Foundation and the British Mountaineering Council thought it was worth supporting and other organisations and companies followed.

Our "planning" meetings such as they were took place in John's front room. It was a place once described by the Editor of the American magazine Climbing, who came to interview Joe some years later, as being bleaker than any expedition base camp. It contained mostly scavenged bits of torn furniture and the threadbare floor was often littered with half-drunk cups of coffee, ash-trays full of cigarette ends and takeaway food wrappers.

It was also the venue for some memorable and outrageous parties. People still recall the occasion when one dancing guest fell through the floor boards and would have landed in the cellar below but for their outstretched arms supporting them as if on thin ice. At another party there was a bonfire in the garden and when the wood supplies got a bit low, the sofa was hauled out of the front room and sacrificed. Sometimes they were a bit much for me and in response to one of John's invitations, I anxiously enquired if it might be more civilised than the previous one and that for example some food might be laid on. John cheerfully said that it would be.

The following Saturday when I turned the corner of his street I saw John standing outside. "See," he said with a smile, pointing at the Kebab van parked on the pavement, "food."

The expedition went well and we had a great adventure. Back in the pub in Sheffield we cheerily recounted how we nearly died many times on and nearly off the Karakoram Highway while being driven from Islamabad to Gilgit, how we put the Base Camp in the wrong valley and had to move it to

access a more climbable side of the mountain and how, whilst it was in the wrong place, the Base Camp was engulfed by an avalanche from a mountain several miles away on the other side of the glacier.

In addition, Andy and John made the first ascent in

good style. Richard and I made an attempt, but Richard's feet became badly blistered on our way from Base Camp to the first bivouac site so the next day he couldn't continue. I went on, bivouacked again and finally reached the col below the summit ridge. Alone on a wide sloping snowfield I became engulfed in cloud, frightened by the idea of falling into unseen crevasses, and couldn't find the snow cave left by Andy and John. I went back down. I was both disappointed and relieved at having an acceptable excuse not to tackle the steep ridge up to the summit unroped on my own.

Joe too was disappointed. He had reached the col with Andy and John, but his damaged knee from his experiences in Peru was giving him a lot of trouble. His frustration was made worse because the fire of his passion for climbing had reignited. He didn't want to give up and Joe famously doesn't give up easily.

Towards the end of the trip I remember lying in one of the tents and sharing thoughts and frustrations about life, climbing and the women in our lives, both present and past, with Joe. We had always got on really well despite being in some ways opposite characters. I think it surprised both of us. Joe, intelligent and insightful, is famously blunt, sometimes selfish and can be quick-tempered. Our biggest areas of common ground were probably our stubbornness and our sense of humour. We usually laughed a lot together. Our roaming conversation was however interrupted on this occasion.

When we entered the tent I was aware that Hugh, a trekker with our team that only Jungle knew, was dozing at the far end. It was only as our conversation continued that I became aware of a small red light glowing at the back. Hugh was secretly tape recording everything we said. I couldn't believe it. Even then I suppose Joe was mildly well known but certainly not the public figure he is today, but that seemed irrelevant, it was a private conversation. Whatever reason he had it seemed creepy and quite inappropriate. I calmly asked him to turn the recorder off and said that if he ever wanted to record other conversations on the trip, he should ask people first. Joe clearly felt the need to put a slightly different emphasis on the point and added that if he ever turned that f***ing thing on again he'd shove it up his f****ing a**e. We also had and still do have a difference in style.

Back home, away from the public reliving of the trip in the pub and elsewhere, I realised that, following Al's death, what had been joy and a growing and sometimes misplaced confidence in my judgement and ability had been supplanted by an equally irrational fear. The fear extended to becoming afraid of getting into a situation when I might feel afraid. To the outside world I might have appeared as normal as usual, but as a climber or mountaineer I felt paralysed by my own emotions.

By the time the summer of 1988 came round things were moving on and healing. Two years had passed since Al had died, I left Sheffield City Council to work freelance as an organisation/management development/training consultant and my then girlfriend Wendy had suggested that we should get married.

We were having a great time together and although I still felt scarred from the breakup of my relationship with Alison only a few years earlier, when asked I couldn't really think of a reason not to. It was probably not a very good reason to do so either though. A normal family life and children did however seem very attractive. It was the end of one era and the beginning of the next, but not as I thought.

In the spring of 1988 Wendy became pregnant and we moved to a larger house; sadly, though, she miscarried.

By the time the summer came everybody else seemed to be going off on a trip somewhere. Joe invited Wendy and me to visit the remote valley of Hushe in the Karakoram with him. The three of us always got on well. Wendy, although widely travelled, had never been to Pakistan and so we would trek and explore and Joe and I would try to climb something together. It would also be Joe's first peak since the Siula Grande climb in Peru. Although Wendy was initially very keen, when the time came to go her heart was not in it, in fact her heart was elsewhere. Her life changed fast in that year. Joe and I climbed a small straightforward peak called Gondoro Peak and the three of us explored the Charakusa Glacier.

Soon after our return to Sheffield, Wendy decided to move out. Some time after we had separated, at the time when the baby would have been born, I felt a deep sense of loss and grieving, probably for many people and things. It was a difficult time.

One evening in the pub in early 1989, Joe confided to me that he really felt that Tupopdan was unfinished business. He suggested that we should go back and give it another go. These days it seems to me to be a bit pointless to return to mountains that you have failed to climb. There are plenty of others to choose from and getting obsessive about things proves little. Nonetheless, in the summer we headed back out to the Karakoram. This time we were a party of four. Janet Moore, a climbing friend of mine from London, joined us and Joe invited his girlfriend and our mutual friend Sue Wallis.

The nearest thing that Sue had experienced in terms of wilderness up to then was some gentle walking in the Peak District. Joe, Janet and I would climb and Sue would trek with us and wait at Base Camp.

This time we thought we had learned from our previous experience. We placed our base camp in the right valley, arranged enough porters to carry our gear and, to avoid previous conflicts, had decided to do all our cooking ourselves. The trek, although only one day, was not straightforward as the route makes a potentially dangerous ascent along a river flanked by vertical rubble (known as conglomerate) walls before reaching the open moraine slopes below the glacier and the mountain itself. The weather in the Karakoram in the summer of 1989 was not good. We experienced rain and snow at our base camp and spent several days huddled in our two Vango tents on a small flat area on the moraines.

When a patch of reasonable weather appeared to be approaching, the three of us set off towards the mountain carrying heavy loads. Our plan was to bivouac on the snow slope where we had previously sited our snow cave in 1987 and then the next day to go for the summit. It was a hot day and it was tiring work breaking trail through the deep soft snow, but eventually we reached a relatively flat area at the lower edge of the glacier in which we could dig a shallow trough, lay out our sleeping bags and mats and settle down for the night.

Joe and Janet both had top of the range down-filled sleeping bags, but with unthinking enthusiasm I had agreed to test a prototype new pile and Pertex bag. It was not up to the job; I was freezing. I spent many hours shivering, shaking the snow off my bag and looking across at the two undulating mounds of Joe and Janet's sleeping bags as they slept peacefully inside, unaware of the gentle snow pattering down upon them.

We planned to start before first light, but even then it was clear that the weather was not good and the slope above us had an accumulation of fresh snow that heightened the risk of an avalanche, particularly if the sun did get on it. Janet and I were for going down and, after some discussion, Joe reluctantly agreed.

It was a long way back down through the soft snow to Sue in the Base Camp. The anticipated storm did not arrive that morning as we thought. In fact the sun shone for a few hours and in the early afternoon the snow slope above our bivouac site avalanched. Who knows, had we continued we might have been on our way down after the avalanche and would have had a safe descent down the slope, or we might not.

The weather did soon break and it poured with rain at base camp. Disheartened, we decided that we would abandon Tupopdan again and go down. As it turned out the return to the road would be the most difficult and dangerous part of the whole trip.

It didn't start well. Our plan was to pack up our camp, descend to the road and hire some porters to walk back up the following day to retrieve our loads. From our previous experience we thought we might even make it down in time for a late lunch, so we travelled light and left all our tents, ropes and equipment in a heap ready for collection. We made a fire and burnt all our rubbish.

As I was feeding some paper into the fire I noticed that someone had thrown a headlamp battery into it. Batteries can explode if burnt and the usual practice is to take them back to a city for disposal so I made a general comment that whoever did it was an idiot and then tried to flick it out with another bit of food packaging.

Suddenly there was a loud explosion and I felt an impact force on my face and tumbled backwards onto the ground. When I came too I was shocked to realise that I was blind. I called out in panic to the others. I was terrified but, rather than the expected rushing over to help, between my panicky gasps of breath I heard hoots of laughter coming from the other three.

The battery had not exploded but a tin of custard powder had and my eyes were sealed over and my clothes covered with the yellow stuff! They thought it was funnier than I did.

Eventually in light rain we set off down towards the river and the gorge that we had previously trekked up. After about 30 minutes we had to make our way along a narrow trail above the now (due to the rain) raging river that ran off the glacier below Tupopdan and under a high unstable conglomerate cliff. I was at the front and saw the stones coming first. Initially it was just small pebbles zinging and bouncing across the trail in front of my steps. I then looked up and could see that a long way above us was a gully down which a torrent of rocks had begun. I called out a warning to the others and ran for the shelter of a large boulder thirty yards ahead.

The others were too far behind to make it. I watched in horror as the barrage came down. Janet behind me was on open ground. At first she dodged out of the way of several of the rocks but there were too many and they were getting bigger. In the end in desperation she improvised the only shelter she could: she took off her expedition rucksack, crouched down behind it and used it as a shield, fending off the onslaught whilst teetering on the edge of the river bank.

Sue had never been in a place anything like this and had no idea what to do. Joe grabbed her round the shoulders as she stood transfixed by the drama and the two of them dodged and dived to avoid the rocks, moving away at the very last second in case the tumbling rocks bounced and changed direction. Any impact would have caused catastrophic injuries. We were in a difficult place and there was no help.

Eventually as I looked up from behind my rock and saw that the deluge had, if not stopped, at least paused, I shrieked to the others to run for it and we all did. Although temporarily we were safe at, least three of us knew that the drama was far from over.

An hour later we were in the main part of a box canyon with vertical conglomerate cliffs rising up on either side of the swollen river as it pounded over the rocks within. It was now raining heavily, increasing the risk of more stonefall, and we were in thick mist. The noise from the water was deafening and you could hear the crashing sound of rocks being dragged and tumbled along in the flow. The whole atmosphere was ominous and added to the general feeling of fear and trepidation. We had crossed the river at this point on the way up and twice in 1987 but today, with it in flood, it was suicide even to attempt it. To reach the road and safety we nonetheless had to.

Joe and I explored several options jumping between rocks and even attempted to wade in the full force of the water. Joe, ever optimistic, kept thinking that there may be a way, but on inspection the gap between the rocks or the force of the torrent was too much. There was no chance. It was still raining and nothing was getting better. We had no option but to wait until the waters went down.

We made an assessment. We didn't have a tent, stove or food and only Joe and I had our sleeping bags with us. Then I remembered seeing a small shepherd's hut some distance away in the other direction on our route to the base camp in 1987. We might be able to find it and it might be habitable enough to give us shelter for long enough for the river level to drop a bit and let us across. We could not think of any other options.

We did find the hut some thirty minutes away and got through the night. Joe and Sue squeezed in one sleeping bag and Janet and I swapped mine by shifts every few hours. We dined on cigarettes, fruit gums and water, but in the morning the rain had eased.

We returned to the river hoping for, but not really expecting the best. The water had dropped a little but it was still very high and thundering down. We still couldn't risk jumping between boulders over the biggest gaps. The chances were that we wouldn't make the jump and, once in the torrent, there would be no way out and we would be swept downstream. We needed a safety back-up. A rope would have been ideal but they were all still back up the mountain at our camp. We decided to improvise. Straps were cut from rucksacks, trouser belts and spare boot laces were called into service. Joe and I explored a possible route. It seemed feasible until the final gap onto the opposite bank. Joe thought he could jump it and from there would use the improvised rope to help everyone across. I thought it was extremely unlikely that he would make it. Joe, in his typical way with a glint in his eye and gesticulating his fingers in a characteristic manner said, "I'll just go and have a look." In my typical way I said that he should not go, and to call me over to confer if it looked possible. I continued to explore another option, but the next thing that I noticed out of the corner of my eye was Joe launching himself off a large block two-thirds of the way across the river, aiming to grab the opposite bank. He didn't make it.

He plunged into the rushing waters, disappearing up to his shoulders, but on surfacing just managed to grab a rock on the bank as he went down. I stood horror-struck and then amazed as moments later Joe hauled himself out of the water and up the bank and gave me a cheery gesture and a big grin of success. Words were impossible against the noise of the river.

Eventually, using the improvised rope everyone got safely across and we stood stunned and relieved that we had made it through.

The remainder of the walk to the settlement at the road was straightforward and only took a few hours. Two days later when the rain and floodwater had stopped a team of porters went back to our camp, collected our gear and returned the same day.

In the end we didn't make the first ascent of the peak suggested by Al, although Andy and John did. We didn't even make the second ascent, although there is a possibility that it is still available to be done. I did however gain a lot from Al's legacy. Amongst other things I learned that I could both experience and achieve things beyond the limitations of my imagination and yet at the same time be disabled or even paralysed by it. I also learned about how empowering letting someone go can be and at the same time how important friendships are. I probably became a slightly better mountaineer too. I only wish Al was still around to enjoy it all.

Chapter 5

From my Dad's Bookshelf

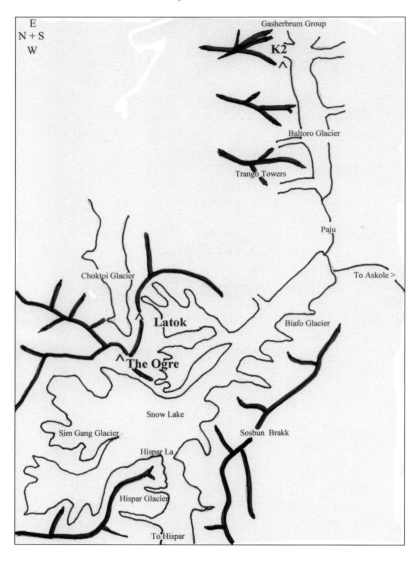

Map of the Biafo, Hispar and Snow Lake Area, Pakistan

For most of his life, except for his time in the Army during the Second World War, my Dad worked in a bank during the week and in his garden at the weekend. In my childhood he led what in today's terms might be described as a risk-averse life, but despite this, deep within him there was also a spark of adventure, although it was mostly played out vicariously. He was for example keen that my brother Rob and I joined the Scouts, was supportive of our early enthusiasm for the hills, and our family holidays were nearly always spent camping, with at least one such trip being to Scotland every year to visit our relatives.

In the bookcase in the living room of our North London semi was also his small collection of mountaineering books. There were the predictable titles of the period, such as John Hunt's account of the 1953 Everest Expedition, but two others caught my attention more. The first was a book simply called

Mountaineering by T.A.H. Peacock. It was the first instruction book I had ever seen on mountaineering. Inside Dad had written his home address, in a small village in the Scottish Borders, and the date of purchase, 8th of March 1943. I never asked him about it but much later it dawned on me that when he wrote it he would probably have been in support of the tanks pursuing Rommel's army across the North African desert. I wondered whether he read it whilst in the desert.

The black and white plates within showed men in tweed jackets, plus fours and wide-brimmed hats demonstrating techniques such as prusiking up and abseiling down ropes or moving roped together along snowy ridges in the Alps. I was captivated by it.

The other book I came to a bit later but it had an even more profound effect on me. It was a shiny, black, thick hardbacked volume with the intriguing title printed in big red letters on the spine. It was *Blank on the Map* by Eric Shipton, published in 1938.* The map that as a result of the expedition filled the blank was attached as a fold-out sheet in the back of the book. I spent many hours studying it, the pictures and the text and trying to work out where, literally, on earth it was. I got out our atlas but just couldn't make head or tail of it.

One thing about which I was sure was that it was in India - it said so in the book - which of course at the time of the expedition, it was. Today (as it was then when I was a not very well-informed teenager) it is in Pakistan. The mystery made the whole thing even more intriguing.

In 1980 Mum and Dad moved out of London into a bungalow in a village in Oxfordshire to be near to Rob, his wife Anne and their new baby. In 1983 I too left London and migrated to Sheffield and didn't give the book much further thought for quite a while.

By the autumn of 1988, after a period of emotional trauma, Wendy left Sheffield, our house and me and moved to Rochdale. I was determined not to be out of my home again and bought her out of her share of our four-bedroom house. Almost out of nowhere came climbing friends who wanted to be lodgers in the house and so began an institution that was known in many parts of the climbing world simply as Steade Road.

One day soon after Wendy had left, Andy Cave, my friend from the first Tupopdan trip, came round for a brew and a chat. In conversation I asked him if he knew anyone who would want to share the house. He said he did - him. He moved in. A few days later a friend from the North London Mountaineering Club arrived. He claimed to be a tax exile from London. We called him Lobby. Some time later again a jovial young new graduate and talented climber, a friend of Andy's, Nick Lewis (from South Wales) moved in too. He became known as the Colossus from the Valleys, or just Colossus for short. Later still, Lobby met and fell in love with Kathleen Jamie, now a renowned Scottish poet, and she moved in too.

One of my fond memories of the period was a perfect weekend in which Lobby, another friend Gary Kinsey and I went up to Scotland in the winter and climbed North Post (Grade 5) on Creag Meagaidh on the Saturday and Crowberry Gully (Grade 4) on the Buachaille on Sunday, all in rare near-perfect conditions. It was a great time.

Rent was mostly paid in money, but on occasions when cash was difficult I received a collection of reggae vinyl records, some repairs to the house, a picture or a poem, all of which lasted much longer than any cash.

The place was also constantly full of other climbers and friends and its reputation kept on spreading. Typically, one winter evening we were sitting watching television when there was a knock on the door. I opened it to see a small, slightly-built chap with two enormous climber's duffle bags. "Hello," he said, "you don't know me but I have your address; my name is Michael and I am from Lodz in Poland. I have come to stay for three months." He did.

He caused a bit of a stir one day when I brought two middle-aged female work colleagues to the house for a meeting. It was, I admit, a misjudgement. Michael from Lodz was doing some pull-ups in the kitchen door frame wearing only his underpants. I think they were sort of impressed. I don't think that sort of thing happened at their homes. Then, having tried to explain the situation to them, we sat down in the living room with the patio doors looking out onto the garden to have our meeting. It was somewhat unfortunate timing that Lobby chose that particular moment to piss on the compost heap. He later explained that the practice was beneficial to making top class compost! I didn't have any more meetings at home after that.

Yet another example of Steade Road's fame was some years later when I was on an expedition in Nepal and I visited a neighbouring group's Base Camp. They were also Eastern Europeans and, as the conversation went on and they learned that I lived in Sheffield, they began talking warmly about the place and how they had visited several times to climb in the Peak District. It turned out that they were regulars at Steade Road but must have stayed there when I was elsewhere.

Food was constantly available for all comers at the house by a system we devised called the "bottomless pit". Lobby had found an old iron cook pot in a skip nearby and had cleaned it up. In it was a constantly evolving casserole of whatever residents or visitors wanted to contribute in the vegetarian line. It seemed to get better and better as the days went on until somebody's nerve would eventually crack and it got emptied and cleaned.

In the summer of 1989 whilst I was engaged on Tupopdan again, Lobby, Andy and a group of friends organised an expedition to climb the unclimbed North Face of the Ogre in Pakistan. The mountain had one previous ascent from the other side by Chris Bonington and Doug Scott in 1977 during which they had an accident near the summit and an epic descent. Access to the North Face was via a different route from the 1977 expedition, crossing the mythical Snow Lake. It was described as being at the heart of the biggest area of glaciation outside the Polar Regions. It was also much to my delight the place described and charted in Eric Shipton's book *Blank on the Map*. I had finally located the infamous Blank.

The team didn't get very far up the Ogre before being driven back by avalanches and bad weather, but they did bring back some fascinating pictures and stories of the peaks and passes around Snow Lake that featured on Shipton's map. Snow Lake is like the centre of an enormous star with five or six massive glaciers bursting outwards from its hub and stretching out right across the western Karakoram. I just had to go, but it would have to wait until the next year. The season had finished and I had to earn some money.

So later during the autumn I found myself working for several clients doing organisation development and training consultancy. One of them was a department of a local university, the Sheffield Business School. They had contracted me to help out on a short residential course based in a hotel in Buxton which served as an introduction to their various Masters in Business Administration (MBA) programmes. On it, much to my surprise, I met the person who very soon became my soul mate, my best friend, the love of my life and later my wife; her name is Janet James.

I was always close to my Mum and she and Janet immediately got on well too. Over the years, Mum had never said anything to try to persuade me not to go to the mountains, but it was always obvious that she was only just holding back tears whenever I saw her before I left on a trip. My selfishness still overcame my guilt about causing her such anxiety. That winter in Oxfordshire, unusually Mum became ill. The GP diagnosed anaemia but, despite not being a doctor, I suspected from the start that she had leukaemia, having witnessed her mother deteriorating with it too. Eventually the doctor also caught on, a proper diagnosis was carried out and Mum began treatment. A slow deterioration was predicted.

The term expedition always seems a bit of a grand name to me, it's a bit like being grown up or middle-aged for that matter. You never really realise that you have reached that stage until you look back on it afterwards. I always just thought about it as going on a mountaineering trip to the Karakoram, but perhaps it was an expedition of a sort.

In terms of formal organisation the trip to Snow Lake certainly didn't follow the traditional route. Inspired as soon as they returned by Andy and Lobby's account, I asked my friend Janet Moore if she fancied going to explore the area; she agreed and that was more or less it. It seemed to me that in the mountains the most effective decision-making unit is two people. In one sense three people make a potentially safer team so if one person has an accident the other two stand a chance of helping, but both the climbing and the decision making will be less efficient. As groups get bigger all sorts of other issues come into play and good decision making gets harder to achieve. As with democracy, if participation is merely the aim, it works, but if good decisions and outcomes are needed, it's not so effective. It could be the drive or ego of one person or just the desire to take charge or it could be that others just abdicate responsibility to avoid conflict. The dynamics can be complex and you never observe them, you are always somehow a part, whether active or passive.

In parallel to us but unknown by us until later many other friends decided to head out to Snow Lake too. By the time we reached Skardu in Northern Pakistan and were arranging for jeeps to take us to the end of the road by the Braldu River, there was quite a mob of us but little formal organisation. Lobby and Kath were there and had brought Kath's younger brother and his friend. Pete Barrass, another climber and close friend from Sheffield, was planning a Grande Climbing Tour starting in Pakistan and continuing into other areas as the season progressed. Pete's friend Fiona Garry (known as Boo) and her boyfriend Paul had recently both graduated and were there too, although Paul had to return early to start a job somewhere. There was also not just one plan; we all had our own. It didn't seem a problem; in fact it seemed like a rather creative solution. We would pool resources when it was helpful and otherwise do our own thing.

Our plan was to trek up the Biafo Glacier to Snow Lake, spend some time exploring the area and hopefully find some easy peaks to have a go at. We would then cross Snow Lake, climb up the pass called the Hispar La and descend the enormous Hispar Glacier to Hispar village. From there we would make a road connection to Gilgit and onwards to Islamabad. Initially we were all delayed reaching the end of the gravel road from Skardu and had to camp for the night at Dassu while a landslide was cleared. The Braldu River, one of the major tributaries of the Indus, is a wild and angry brown-coloured river. If you stand on its banks, in addition to the roaring water you can hear huge boulders being dragged and crashed along under the surface and feel the vibration of all the forces in the ground beneath your feet. In the end the gravel trail wasn't completely cleared and we finished up walking some of the distance.

A few years before, on an expedition with the legendary Sheffield mountaineer Paul Nunn, Pat Fearneough, one of the team members, had been swept off his feet by a small gravel landslide here and shockingly disappeared for ever into the Braldu in full view of his friends.

These days there is a road bridge that crosses the Braldu and gives access to the village of Askole, but in 1990 everything had to be hauled across in a tiny wooden box which was suspended from a pulley on a cable. The box was just about big enough to take one person, a rucksack and a goat at a time and so the whole process of getting all of us and the locals, who had also all arrived with a herd of goats, took some time. If the rope pullers needed a rest whilst you were mid-channel, looking down at the wild, swirling, milky tea-coloured waters below was just as daunting and nauseating as clinging on to the petrified goat whose face was against yours and whose hooves were desperately trampling your lap.

Askole is not a nice place. It is very remote and despite considerable amounts of aid over the years things don't look much better even now. I think the basic problem is perhaps that the gene pool is just too small. On the plus side there are some nice hot springs not far away and they provided the last proper bathing opportunity for us for quite some time.

We trekked up the Biafo Glacier from Askole in three delightful days. The scenery become more and more dramatic at every turn and, much to my relief but also slightly worryingly, we saw no signs of the large brown bear that had troubled trekkers and climbers alike in the area for several years. Whilst obviously not wanting to be attacked by a bear that could allegedly split a plastic barrel open with its claw, I really didn't want it to have been shot either.

At the edge of Snow Lake we made our Base Camp. Towering above us was the magnificent twin-summited peak of Susbun Brakk (6413m) and away at the far end of Snow Lake on the Sim Gang Glacier ahead of us was the North Face of

Baintha Brakk, otherwise known as the Ogre (7285m).

Janet wasn't feeling too well so after a few days of rest and acclimatisation I went to try to tackle one of the small peaks on the other side of the glacier with Pete. The plan was to climb in the dark to get the best freezing conditions on the snow and ice. We were both going well and soon crossed Snow Lake and began working our way up the crevassed section of the glacier that led towards a small summit, Pete being in front. The crevasses became increasingly complex however and eventually we found ourselves in a cul de sac. We couldn't cross the crevasses as they were either too wide or the step up to reach them was too high, or both. The only possible way was back the way we had come. I t was a disappointing excursion.

A few days later the party split. Most people went back via Askole as some needed to return to the UK, others didn't fancy crossing the Hispar La and committing to the long trek down the other side carrying all our kit. Janet was not recovering as quickly as she had hoped so opted for descent too.

Four of us - Lobby, Pete, Boo and me - set off for the Hispar La with full climbing and camping kit and food for a few days. Lobby, despite being very experienced and having been to the area before, wasn't going very well and was apparently struggling with either illness, altitude or both. We trekked up to the Hispar La roped up together.

Our first camp was on top of the Hispar La and our aim was to attempt to climb Workman Peak the next day. The peak was given its name by the first ascentionists Fanny Bullock Workman and her husband during, amazingly, one of their eight Himalayan expeditions between 1898 and 1912 (a truly astonishing achievement then and pretty impressive now). Unfortunately the weather broke during the night and we had little time, so we had no option but to begin our trek down the Hispar.

The others had planned to meet us in Gilgit on a predetermined day, giving us just enough time to complete the trip.

Everybody recalls things differently, even if they are witness to the same experience, but certainly what happened over the next few days retells now as strange and would be easy to criticise from an outside observer's point of view. As a participant my feelings then and now are that we made the best decisions we could at the time to look after ourselves and others but only just got away with it. It is a bit like asking a local person for instructions on how to get somewhere and they respond that if they were going there, they wouldn't start from here.

Somehow, despite everyone being good friends for many years, a bit of tension had built up over the preceding days between Pete and Lobby. It's hard to know what it was about. Perhaps it was a battle for who should have been in charge? Maybe someone should have been? Who knows? There certainly was an atmosphere in our small group as we left the Hispar La.

The initial descent was straightforward and as we dropped down the few hundred metres from the pass we could see the view all the way down the Hispar Glacier. Mostly it was strewn with boulders with ridges of ice poking through in places, interspersed with areas of flatter bare ice and crevasses. Either side it was hemmed in by near-vertical conglomerate cliffs above which small ablation valleys ran parallel to the glacier. Above that sheer mountains closed in tightly on either side. The highest peak in the area is the little known giant Kunyang Chhish at 7852m.

Lobby was a few hundred metres ahead. I was just ahead of Pete and Boo, who were further back studying the view from the knoll. Lobby wanted to take a line to the side of the glacier. To the rest of us the direct line down the centre seemed a better option. A brief conversation was shouted across the glacier with various arm gestures by both parties encouraging the other to go the way they wanted. Lobby was on the brink of entering a boulder field and Pete and Boo were high on the knoll above.

Neither appeared to want to concede and as it was a simple choice of one route or the other, there wasn't much room for a compromise either. After a short communication, Lobby gestured his arms and shoulders into resignation, turned and disappeared into the boulder field. Some shouting followed to try to call him back, but sound doesn't travel well in such terrain. I wondered whether I should rush after him and then at least we would be two parties of two in case anything went wrong. I thought it was quite likely that I would never find him amongst the boulders though and would by then have to make my own way down alone. I also thought that the way straight down the glacier route looked safer and quicker.

The three of us stayed on the knoll for a while to see if we could spot Lobby's red pack moving in the boulder field, but we couldn't. I felt that I had been in an impossible position that was not of my own making, but if anything happened to Lobby it would be my fault. We eventually set off on rocky but straightforward terrain down the glacier, camped comfortably that night and set off again in the morning.

On the second day the easiest line down the ice seemed to trend towards the right bank as we saw it. Eventually it drew us rather scarily right underneath the near-vertical conglomerate walls that flanked the glacier. In many places they were more than 50 metres high and as we descended they reached even higher.

Late on in the afternoon of the second day Pete and I were at the front and Boo was just a short way (still in speaking distance) behind. The conglomerate wall was not straight, but rather waved in and out creating a winding route for our trail. At one point I looked back and saw Boo disappear into one of these inlets. I said to Pete that we should wait. We did. She didn't appear. We thought that maybe she had gone to the toilet. We waited, she still didn't appear, so we began to retrace our steps. We found Boo's boot marks, but to our amazement she had disappeared. We couldn't understand it; she had been so close she couldn't have just disappeared. In a state of anxiety we checked all the nearby crevasses and followed our route back some distance, but found nothing. What could have happened? Then it got dark.

Pete and I bivouacked on the glacier and resumed our search at first light. We went back to the place where we had seen her boot prints and on close inspection noticed that they made an unlikely series of steps directly up the cliff from where we stood. We followed them up the steep wall and eventually they and we reached a wide grassy pasture of an ablation valley that was clearly used by villagers from Hispar for grazing their animals. What a sense of relief: at least she was safe, although there was still no sign of Lobby!

Carefully tracking her footsteps we followed a series of goat tracks until another glacier, the Kunyang, crossed our path before joining the Hispar. Again we were able to follow Boo's boot prints down the steep zigzag goat trail to join the glacier. Once on the glacier there were no more tracks as the route went over boulders and large rocks. On reaching the other side, however, our anxiety rose again as we could not find her tracks on the goat trail back up the other side. We looked up and down the Kunyang Glacier and then climbed to the top of the trail to get a better view. There was no sign of Boo. We had lost her and then found her and now lost her again.

From my Dad's Bookshelf

There was a horrifying possibility that only two out of the four of us were going to make it back to Hispar. The trail on the other side was easier and we even met a local man with a mule. I paid him a few rupees to take my pack and we all trekked together down into Hispar Village.

On reaching Hispar we soon noticed the familiar outline of Lobby sitting alone on the porch in front of the tiny school building. He had only been there an hour. It was great to see him and it seemed to me that somehow the past few days had taken the pressure out of the tension between him and Pete. fter a brief reunion we were soon returned to gloom, though, as Boo had still not been seen.

From the school building you could get a clear view back up the Hispar Glacier. It was absolutely massive. You could hide things the size of houses amongst the boulders and rubble. The chance of seeing Boo was minimal. Also the moraine conglomerate walls that flanked both sides of the glacier were now enormous and there was little chance of climbing up them safely.

Sitting and waiting also didn't seem like a very good option so, leaving Lobby and Pete at Hispar to wait, I set off walking to the road-head in the hope that I could get a message back to the others in Gilgit,or at least to our hotel and ask them to send a jeep. I wondered whether it would be taking three or four passengers or if we'd be using it to recruit a search team. To my delight, as I approached the road-head I heard a jeep revving up to leave. I ran as best I could in plastic boots and with a big pack and gave the driver a note and explained the situation. As he disappeared off down the dusty road, I wasn't very confident that anything would happen.

Again I was torn. Should I be in Hispar if Boo was injured and we needed to carry her, or should I have gone to Gilgit to

103

make sure the jeep driver delivered the message? What good could I do just waiting at the road-head? The irrational truth was that I didn't want to leave without knowing what had happened to Boo. I got out my Karrimat and my cotton sheet sleeping bag liner and got in it to keep both the heat and flies at bay. They were long hours of waiting.

Late the next morning I heard voices and then Lobby, Pete and Boo suddenly rounded the corner. Boo was fine but had had an amazing adventure. She had been unable to find the trail up from the Kunyang Glacier and so had been making her way down the Hispar but had been unable to climb up the conglomerate wall and get off. She had tried to climb up several times but had fallen off, fortunately without injury. She had even abandoned all her gear except her jacket, empty rucksack and good luck mini teddy bear. As if by magic, and with perfect timing, almost as soon as the story had been retold, a jeep arrived with a driver looking for Mr Tom and his friends.

Some hours later we arrived in the rain at the small town of Gilgit. It was great to see familiar shops and houses again and even better to spot two figures walking grim faced up the main street. It was Kath and Janet. They had not received any news of our whereabouts and only knew that we were several days late.

After a rest, food and a lot of talking, the next day Janet and I jumped aboard a local mini bus and headed back down the Karakoram Highway to catch our plane home. Lobby and Kath were planning to stay in the area for a while, exploring further before returning to the UK. Pete planned to head off on his next trip.

When Lobby and Kath returned from a few days of exploration they were confused to find Pete's hotel room door open and all his possessions inside, but no sign of him. Over the ensuing few days Pete had begun to feel ill and as he didn't seem to be getting better (in fact he felt like he was deteriorating fast), he admitted himself to Gilgit hospital. Gilgit hospital was not good and Pete was left deteriorating further on a makeshift bed in the sweltering heat. Eventually Lobby and Kath found him in both a poor physical condition and in very poor medical conditions, barely conscious. Pete was not really able to look after himself by this stage. Lobby and Kath packed his gear and skilfully got him onto one of the few tiny planes that fly to and from Islamabad (weather permitting).

Once Pete eventually got back to the UK, he was admitted to hospital in Sheffield and spent many weeks being treated.

On my return to Heathrow, Janet was there to meet us. It was really great to see her, but she brought terrible news. Instead of the slow decline in Mum's health that had been predicted, things had deteriorated very quickly. Mum was in John Radcliffe Hospital in Oxford with the rest of the family at her bedside. I rang the hospital from the Arrivals area. The nurse said that my Mum had just died a few minutes before. Apparently she had asked what the time was and, having been told, said that my plane should have landed and that I would be home safely. Then she died.

*See *Six Mountain Travel Books*, Eric Shipton, <u>The Mountaineers/ Baton Wicks,</u> 1985.

Chapter 6

Visits to the Unmarried Daughter

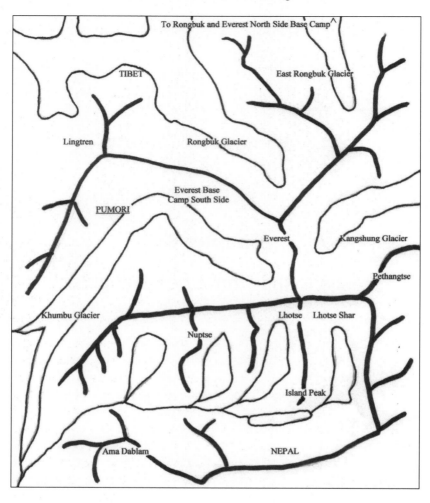

Map of Pumori and the Khumbu Peaks

Joe Simpson was on a roll. Since our two unsuccessful trips to Tupopdan in Pakistan his passion for mountaineering had been rekindled and was now ablaze. He was working for a guiding company and it seemed to me that he was also going on as many trips with friends as he could. Towards the end of 1990 he and his friend Mal Duff hatched a plan to climb a new route on a relatively small peak in the Khumbu Area of Nepal called Parchamo. Mal, as well as being a very accomplished climber and developer of new routes across Scotland and the Himalaya, was also one of the first of what could be called Himalayan Guide Entrepreneurs. He guided groups of paying clients up Himalayan peaks. He was a decade or more ahead of his time with his idea of commercial Himalayan guiding.

Mal and Joe's plan was to advertise the proposed trip to other interested climbers and trekkers as a way of reducing the overall cost. They placed an advertisement in High Magazine and awaited the response. Next to their advert in the classified section was a notice from the climbing equipment manufacturers and distributors Troll. They were recalling their Grivel 2F model of crampons because there was a potential fault that in some situations might lead to the crampons coming off the toe of the boots. We all had Grivel 2F crampons.

I was lucky, I discovered the problem with mine on easy ground descending from Creag Meagaidh with Lobby. Mal discovered it with his when he began to descend from the summit of Parchamo having achieved a first ascent. Both Joe and Mal, roped together, fell together. Joe described the scene that as one of them managed to get a brake in with their ice axe the other would accelerate past and pull them off. Joe once again incurred major injuries, this time to his left ankle, head and face and together and injured they had to spend a night out on the mountainside. The next day Joe was helped down by Mal and our mutual friend Chhwang and other Sherpas, who carried him to a place of safety from where he could be helicoptered to Kathmandu for medical treatment.

Mal's next entrepreneurial endeavour was to climb a mountain near Everest nicknamed the Unmarried Daughter (of Everest - although some people claim that it referred to his own daughter) by no less than George Mallory when he viewed it from Tibet. It is still known by the Sherpa language translation which is Pumo Ri (7161m). Again Mal advertised for clients and recruited a small group of four Brits and one Icelander. Joe suggested that he and I should go along at cost price just to fill the numbers on the permit and that we could have a go at climbing it together. It is a big mountain with a big reputation. It was first climbed by a German expedition in 1962 but had had several ascents and claimed several lives since, mainly due to a relatively high avalanche and falling ice risk on the middle slopes. Pumo Ri was undoubtedly a beautiful and attractive daughter as well as a dangerous one.

The main group made an extended acclimatisation trek in to the Base Camp. I was delayed by the small detail of having to earn a living but flew out as soon as I could to meet them. Mal sent one of his local support team down to the airstrip at Lukla to meet me. The man who met me was called Arjun Gurung. He was an unusual person to be in this role. Ethnically he was not a Sherpa, but a Gurung from Western Nepal. Due to his father being in a senior post in the Nepalese Army he had also had the benefit of being educated at a private boarding school in Calcutta. However, he left before the final exams by cabling a request for his father to send more money for a text book. When it arrived, he spent it on a ticket home (much to the displeasure of his parents, I'm sure).

Arjun was a friendly, charming and intelligent young man and due to his education he spoke perfect English. In many ways however he was an outsider. Ethnically he was not one of the Sherpas and, as the oldest son in his middle class Nepali family, was not meeting with their approval by not living up to their hopes and expectations for him either.

Little did I know it at the time, but Arjun would both directly and indirectly have a significant impact on my life for many years.

We trekked up through the Khumbu following the traditional Everest Base Camp Trail and arrived in Pumo Ri Base Camp about a week after the rest of the party. I was soon shocked to learn that Mal, his wife Liz and one of the clients, Mark Wareham, were already coming down from the summit. Joe and the other clients were in the Camp. It all seemed a bit confusing.

Joe was stomping, or rather hobbling about in an understandable rage of frustration. Due to the Parchamo accident, despite various operations, treatments and physiotherapy he was still walking painfully on crutches. For most people having made the trek to Base Camp would have been a great achievement in itself, but understandably it just made it worse for Joe. He obviously would not be fit enough to climb and was generally disgruntled about the bad luck that seemed to follow him. I had always said to him when we discussed the accusation by others that he was accident-prone that I disagreed. I said he was in fact survival-prone. Most people would not have made it through even one of his misadventures.

Joe decided that enough was enough and the same morning that I arrived he headed off on his crutches in the direction of home. Even with Joe gone there was still a certain amount of frustration at Base Camp. To the other paying clients who were not experienced climbers it was pretty obvious that Mal would not be strong enough to climb the mountain again or even twice more to guide them up. The next morning, Mal, Liz and Mark were still descending and so the Icelander Ari Gunnerson packed up his gear and headed up the mountain, despite advice from me to the contrary. He planned to make a lightweight ascent of the mountain alone. One of his reasons for coming to Pumo Ri he said was to climb the mountain as a memorial to two other Icelandic climbers, friends of his in the small community of Icelandic Mountaineers who were killed in an avalanche just below the summit in 1989. It seemed like a bad idea to me and it has always struck me that to climb anything to prove something is likely to distort your mountaineering judgements and lead to inappropriate decisions. Sometimes that is even true when the goal is just that you really want to prove that you can get to the summit; you can get summit fever and make the wrong call.

I really like Yvonne Chouinard's remark in his book *Let My People Go Surfing** when he says, "Many people don't understand that how you climb a mountain is more important

112

than reaching the top." I would add that why you do it is pretty important too.

Ari did make it to the summit but low down on his descent was killed by a chunk of falling ice 50 metres from the second camp. It knocked him over and made him drop his axe. He slid, tumbled and then fell through the air for several hundreds metres to his death. Despite a search his body was never recovered from the tangle of rock and ice below. He wasn't wearing a helmet or a harness to attach himself to the fixed lines (Mal and I subsequently found them in his tent) and apparently he didn't have a leash on his ice axe, but in the end, having them might not have been enough to save him either. Using my ice hammer and a rock peg I spent a day making a memorial stone for Ari at Base Camp. It was also a reminder, almost a plea in the hope that the same thing might not happen again. Apparently, it's still there.

Of the remaining clients, two of them (both serving Police Officers) were still keen to do something, although they rightly concluded that Pumo Ri was not only dangerous, but way out of their league. Despite not being there in any guiding capacity I offered to take them to explore some of the small peaks and passes in the area that we could see on the other side of the Khumbu Glacier. We trekked around to the opposite side of these mountains and climbed up to just below a high pass called the Kongma La and camped. For me it was a delight. I had never been there before and there was little information about the area, despite it being only a few miles from the busy Everest Base Camp trekking trail. Peaks in Nepal according to the Government are classified into different groups. The title Trekking Peak is a confusing one given to those on a list of mountains rising to nearly six and a half thousand metres and pretty much all of which can not be trekked up. Many are very attractive peaks and some have defeated even the strongest of climbers. One of their main attractions is that they do not have the financial and bureaucratic restrictions that permission for other expedition peaks requires. At the time the only documentation that was widely available about them was the book *The Trekking Peaks of Nepal* by Bill O'Connor**. Even today no one person has climbed all the original list of 14 Trekking Peaks and the list has more than doubled in number now.

We attempted to climb a couple of these relatively small peaks. The first was called Kongma Tse. Despite reaching the rather loose and rocky summit ridge the others didn't want to continue, so we turned back. Then we climbed a long, narrow, spiky rock traverse that eventually led to the summit of another peak called Pokalde. The climbing wasn't especially difficult but climbing any rock at high altitude in double plastic boots isn't easy. It reminded me how delightful exploration mountaineering can be and I discovered how satisfying sharing the adventure with Mal's clients was too, in a way that set me on a path for the future.

The next day I was keen to continue my explorations and so set off alone to cross the Cho La, a glacier-covered pass that links the Everest Trail with Gokyo. Today it is a popular route for more adventurous commercial trekking parties, but in 1991 I was alone. I bivouacked on the open hillside that night and then continued down a less trekked trail to Tengboche Monastery. Tengboche is one of the most important monasteries in the strongly Buddhist Khumbu Region and certainly has one of the best views of the Everest Range. At the time of this visit however it was being rebuilt. A new head Monk or Lama had been appointed and was horrified to realise that the whole of the ancient building was lit only using yak butter candles. It was a huge fire risk. He arranged for a small, new petrol-driven generator to be carried all the way from Kathmandu to provide electric lighting. The trek took several weeks. Unfortunately, soon after the generator's installation in 1989, because of a wiring fault the whole place burnt down!

Visits to the Unmarried Daughter

The following morning just after dawn, in contrast to my few days alone in the wilderness, I witnessed one of the most commercial stunts on Everest up to that time. It was organised by the famous mountaineer Russell Brice and featured Eric Jones and film maker Leo Dickinson. That morning I saw for the first and probably last time ever two hot air balloons fly over the summit of Everest to land in Tibet.

Back in Kathmandu Arjun suggested a plan. He and I could both set up businesses to bring people to trek and climb in Nepal. I would deal with the UK end and he would do everything in Nepal. It seemed like an exciting idea. I thought I would build things up gradually. The whole thing however very nearly ended before it had even begun. The first trip in the autumn of 1992 might not have happened at all if we had taken a flight a couple of days earlier. Our friends from Sheffield, Mark Miller and Victor Radvils, had boarded a flight in Pakistan having just finished a climbing trip in the Karakoram. Another group, instructors and friends from Plas Y Brenin (the National Mountain Centre in Snowdonia) had flown from Britain and changed planes in Pakistan on their way to Nepal to climb the South face of Annapurna 1. Only minutes from landing, the plane flew into a hillside in thick cloud some miles short of its destination in Kathmandu. All passengers and crew were killed and debris was spread over a wide area. For me, as well as trying to cope with the loss, it was particularly shocking and confusing that so many able mountaineers had died, powerless to do anything, on one of the safest stages of their adventures that autumn.

The evening before my own departure, just after the crash I received an anxious telephone call from Joe. He had miscalculated and had thought that I was on the fatal flight. For several reasons he was relieved that I answered the phone and he didn't have to ask Janet the most difficult of difficult questions or, even worse, leave a voice mail message enquiring whether I was dead or not.

The first trip went very well and Arjun did a great job. I had brought a group of people I had known through work and we trekked in an unfrequented area near Gorkha, rafted down the Trisuli River and visited the wildlife in Chitwan National Park.

Interest grew and over the next three years I brought more and more clients to either trek or climb some of the Trekking Peaks. Arjun was not a climber but on one occasion he climbed to just below the top of one of them (Island Peak) with us.

As time went on though I became more and more concerned about him. Alcoholism and just plain heavy drinking, particularly of locally made alcohol called chang and rakshi is quite common in Nepal. It is particularly so amongst young men who work for cash during the trekking season and have nothing to do during the monsoon except to drink and gamble. Arjun had always enjoyed a drink, but the habit was becoming more and more of a problem. His choice was not the cheap and relatively weak local brews, but imported vodka. It also later became clear that he wasn't being fair with money that should have been paid to trek staff for salaries or to his wife for running their modest one-room home.

As with other addictions, the people who suffer from them will promise all sorts of things and will swear that they will do what is required of them. Being either naive or, as I'd rather see it, an optimist, I am inclined to believe them and give them the benefit of the doubt. Clearly, though, Arjun was deteriorating. We were friends and it was painful to see him and his situation get worse at every visit. I felt mostly sad for his wife Nima and their lovely, lively young daughter Anita who was doing really well at the local primary school. Whatever else, they needed Arjun to keep working to bring in the money to live.

Pumo Ri, like Tupopdan some years before, niggled

116

away at Joe and for 1996 he came up with a complex scheme - a campaign, even. He suggested another expedition but, unlike those of previous years, it would be quite big. There were to be two parties.

Joe would be the leader of a four person team comprising Ray Delaney, Ric Potter and Dr Ian "Tat" Tattersall, and my long-time friend Richard Haszko would be the leader of another five person team comprising Tony Halliwell, Bruce French, Steve Hartland, Karen Grunberg and myself. We would climb the Normal Route, the way I had hoped to climb in 1991(the South-East Face and North-East Ridge) and Joe and his team would attempt a steep and unclimbed route on the South Face overlooking the Khumbu glacier that Joe had spotted in 1991 and had called the South Pillar.

Arjun was desperately keen that he should deal with all the organisation and arrangements for the expedition. It would, he claimed, be his big break into organising expeditions which would also make him more financially secure, or at least give him a bigger income. It was tricky. I knew he had been capable of doing a great job just a few years earlier but he would really have to up his game for Pumo Ri. I helped him as much as possible but didn't fancy being the leader of the Normal Route Team as I wasn't living in the UK at the time and also mostly I didn't fancy being torn between Joe and Arjun if they couldn't work together, although I had no inkling that things would go quite as badly as they did.

As a rather big bit of acclimatisation before Pumo Ri, Joe and I decided we would fly west to Pokhara, trek into the Annapurna Sanctuary and make a traverse of Tarpu Chuli and Singu Chuli, otherwise known as Tent Peak and Fluted Peak, by climbing the connecting ridge between the two of them. It was to be just the two of us with no fixed ropes or camps to ease a retreat. It was a big commitment and, in addition it was still a little early in the season and the monsoon had not quite finished. We shrugged this second problem off by rationalising that the situation back in 1985 had been similar and Richard, Martin, Phurba and I had got up Tent Peak alright then. Joining us was a mutual friend, Ali Reynolds from London, who happened to be out there on holiday in Nepal. She would come along for the trek.

The flight from Kathmandu to Pokhara is supposed to be memorable because of the magnificent views of the Himalaya from the right side of the plane. For me it was memorable as being one of those occasions when you just can't stop laughing. If it hadn't been for the seat belts we would have been on the floor. It wasn't that any particular thing made us laugh, just everything did. It was brilliant. It felt really good to be going climbing again with my friend Joe.

It was also good to return to a now familiar area. I had of course visited it with Richard, Martin and Phurba a decade earlier, but I had also climbed Tent Peak again in the late autumn of 1995, this time via the Normal Route with another Sherpa friend called Rahar while a group of trekking friends had a rest day at Annapurna Base Camp far below. It had been a swift and delightful excursion. The glacier was easy and the snow ribs up the headwall offered perfect solid névé so we cramponed up to the narrow summit ridge in no time. As we moved together along it towards the small final summit the sun blazed, but moments later it darkened slightly as we experienced a rare partial lunar eclipse. We stood transfixed on the summit for twenty minutes before descending in a similar efficient style. It was a round trip of four hours from our high camp, mountaineering perfection.

The whole area was changing fast. The Annapurna Conservation Project had been created and it had generated improved paths and lodges and there were many more trekkers about. In Chomrong, for old time's sake, the three of us stayed

118

at the Captain's Lodge. The Captain was still there, although older and physically frailer than when I last met him. I thought his days of chasing miscreants with his shotgun and kukri knife were over, although his spirit showed no sign of fading.

We reached the place called Annapurna Base Camp (it is not where an expedition to climb Annapurna 1 would site its Base Camp, but it is a great trekking destination) and prepared ourselves for the long trek across the South Annapurna Glacier and up to the High Camp. It was about as modest as was possible - just one tiny single skin Gore-Tex Gemini tent with the two of us and all our kit and supplies crammed in. That night it snowed. When the weather cleared we set off up and across the glacier. We were carrying large loads, were roped up and moved cautiously across the fresh snow-covered ice unable to see any but the most obvious crevasses. When we reached the base of the headwall it was clear that it had accumulated a lot of snow. Joe made an attempt to lead off up the first pitch, but it was soon obvious that we were going nowhere. The soft snow just didn't take any weight. If it was that bad low down, it would only get worse higher up. After floundering for a while Joe offered me a go at the lead. I courteously declined.

A pit dug in the snow revealed a high avalanche risk, as if we didn't know it already. We had no choice but to retrace our steps back to camp and think again. That evening, huddled in the tent, we discussed what to do. We had several days of food and to me the weather now seemed to be improving, so perhaps in a day or two we might be able to get up something or just explore the area a bit more. Joe on the other hand wasn't keen and was all for heading back down first thing in the morning. For Joe it was all or nothing.

We failed to reach a compromise and the next morning Joe headed off down. Little spats between friends are just a part of life but back in Kathmandu several things took a turn for

119

the worse and exacerbated everything.

Richard, as the leader of the "Normal" route team, soon arrived. He and Joe (leader of the proposed new South Pillar route team), had a meeting with the life long Kathmandu resident and world renowned mountaineering journalist Elizabeth Hawley*** as all expedition leaders do. Liz, as she is known to her friends, has kept the most complete record of mountaineering achievements in Nepal for many decades and always has the most up-to-date information about peaks, routes and climbers.

She immediately took the wind out of Joe's sails by informing him that his proposed new route had in fact already been climbed by two Czech climbers. Joe was shocked, angry, disappointed and, I think, a bit embarrassed. The rest of his team would be arriving any time and he guessed that none of them would be satisfied with trying to make a second ascent of "their" route or be particularly interested in the more popular Normal Route. Liz also said that there were a couple of other groups on the Normal Route and, due to recent heavy snowfall, a lot of avalanches too.

Things then became further compounded by Arjun. We had anticipated that he, as is normal for the person who has the job of Sirdar, would trek with us and arrange the flights and yak transport of the gear and supplies to the base camp. He would also stay there organising and overseeing everything for the duration of the expedition and be our communication with the outside world to ensure that our rubbish was correctly disposed of and to make contact with Kathmandu if, for example, a rescue helicopter needed to be organised. To that end, to help him and the kitchen staff a bit I had brought from home a load of extra warm kit including a sleeping bag and down jackets. I took them round to the small single room in which he lived with his wife Nima and daughter Anita in the suburbs of Kathmandu. When he opened the door he told me straightaway that he wasn't coming on the expedition because he was sick. He said he had TB. I had no way of knowing whether that was true or not, although I did have my doubts, but it struck me that rather like the opportunity he had been given by his father for a high quality education in Calcutta, he had intentionally or perhaps otherwise again blown his big chance.

Over the following few days I visited Arjun several times. I'm not sure whether I was trying to resolve my doubts about his condition (he was not bedridden and I never saw any medication - which would have been very expensive to buy anyway) or just wanted to try to persuade him that, assuming the TB wasn't real, he really should fulfil his commitment to the expedition. I suppose the problem was that if he hadn't been telling the truth, once you have started on a direction, you have to keep up the story. It is very difficult to backtrack and still have any credibility.

Arjun had been paid various amounts of money for permits, a mandatory Liaison Officer, internal flights and the purchase of supplies etc, so it would therefore not at that stage have been possible to just move to another agent either. He told me that he had asked Chhwang Sherpa, a friend of both Joe and me, to step in and do the job. Chhwang was in fact the Sirdar of the group of Sherpas who carried and helped Joe down from Parchamo when he had his accident with Mal Duff. To that extent he was an excellent choice. Chhwang was also a bit perplexed by the whole situation. He also could only agree to come with us and get the Base Camp set up, but could not stay for the whole expedition because he had his own business commitments elsewhere. It didn't help either that shortly before the expedition Arjun had asked me if a friend of his, called Karen Grunberg from Germany, could join our group. I tried to avoid even being the conveyor of the request but in the end passed it on to Richard as the leader. I had met Karen once in Namche Bazaar after she had climbed Ama Dablam. I liked her, she was obviously strong and spoke perfect English, but was perhaps perceived as an outsider and linked to Arjun and therefore me by the rest of the team.

Altogether the situation wasn't looking good. I felt confused, disappointed, isolated and yet somehow responsible. I was being accused of all sorts of failures, misjudgements and shortcomings separately by Arjun and Joe. I couldn't have anticipated all that happened and most of it was not my responsibility, but I have to concede that at the very least I was naive and over-optimistic that things would just work out. The atmosphere was not good. Generally speaking, all these years later I still have the same fault, if it is one: I am still inclined to optimism and to expect the best of people.

Janet was in Kathmandu visiting me between trips. At the time we lived in Dhaka in Bangladesh, so it was only a short flight away and a weekend visit to Kathmandu was not that unusual. I discussed the whole thing with her endlessly. I very nearly decided just to abandon the whole expedition and my emotional and financial commitment to it and go back home with her. Perhaps I should have?

Eventually the rest of the team arrived. Joe had already updated the South Pillar group by fax that their new route had been climbed so they were by then resigned and philosophical about things. Privately I clung on to the mantra that "everything would be all right once we got on the mountain".

By the time we all reached Base Camp however my mantra was still showing few signs of working. "Tat", a GP from near Manchester had developed a chest infection that would in due course count him out of the entire expedition. Steve Hartland, a climbing instructor at Plas Y Brenin, was also sick with what was confirmed by the staff at the medical post at Pheriche as a pulmonary oedema. He rested in Pheriche and

I rather thought that we would not see him again during the trip. Certainly if I had been diagnosed with such a potentially life-threatening problem, even when I had technically recovered from it I might well be inclined to go back to Kathmandu as soon as possible. Ric, left without a climbing partner, joined the Normal Route team, leaving just Joe and Ray to tackle the South Pillar. The snow conditions on the mountain looked deep and avalanche-prone as we had been warned by Liz Hawley in Kathmandu and the weather as far as we could interpret it from the clouds above did not look like it was going to get much better soon either.

After a few days of acclimatisation walks and intermittent snow, we eventually all began our tasks. Joe and Ray started to explore and work their way up their route and the rest of us set up a camp at the base of the Normal Route and began fixing ropes up the snow and rock ridge above. One of the nice things about climbing as a group of friends can be that, unlike in a traditional siege expedition with an appointed leader and a plan, people contribute in the best way they can. Between us all, without any central plan, over a few days we had soon fixed the ropes and established a dump of gear at the top of the ridge. The ridge itself was quite interesting, steepening and contorting towards the top. The final few rope lengths required a slightly delicate rightward traverse that led to a narrow snow fin. Either side it dropped steeply away, giving in one direction a clear view straight down to our Base Camp and in the other, farther away on the other side, Everest Base Camp at the base of the Khumbu Glacier. Intimidated by the drop I could never quite bring myself to walk along the top of the fin despite there eventually being a fixed rope along it. I always had to shuttle along one flank of it, front pointing on my crampons in a crablike fashion.

The top of the ridge would be the site of the next camp and it also marked the beginning of the huge but mostly relatively easy-angled face that leads to the northern shoulder of Pumo Ri. The face is one of the most dangerous parts of the mountain. It is mostly a vast sheet of glacial ice. During bad weather it accumulates large quantities of snow. As the snow builds up it gets progressively more dangerous both from small avalanches (triggered by local conditions such as falling ice or climbers moving ahead) and massive ones where, as the structure of the snow pack changes, the whole slope, nearly half the side of the mountain, could form an enormous slab avalanche. I was very conscious that it was as he approached this spot on the lower part of the face that Ari Gunnerson was killed by a falling chunk of ice back in 1991.

Some days later, Karen and I hauled loads up the ridge and pitched a tent on the snow at the end of the fixed ropes. Our plan was to gain some acclimatisation by sleeping at the camp and then to go down to rest before returning to push on the route up the face. As we were putting the final touches to securing the tent in this isolated and amazing spot, I was surprised to see a single figure confidently moving along the top of the ice fin and heading towards us. It turned out to be Steve Hartland. He was apparently fully recovered and, although a bit wearied by the sudden height gain, was going well. The three of us squeezed in the tent and spent the night up there.

During the next break in the weather, Karen and I again climbed the fixed ropes to spend another night in the camp. Some very strong climbers have made the summit and back in a single push from the camp, but I felt that another camp at the top of the face on the summit ridge would be less committing. The next day was to be one of reconnaissance. In the morning Karen wasn't feeling well so I said that I would go up the face a bit to see what the conditions were like. If she felt okay we could spend a further night at the camp and move up the next day.

I set off in the cold and dark, but even then the snow

was soft and not fully frozen overnight. Higher up it would be increasingly dangerous. I moved slightly higher up and the snow became deeper. At every step I sunk to my knees. It was clear that I wasn't going far that day. I stopped for a breather, gasping in the thin air, and dug a hole in the snow to study the layers and to get a better idea of the risks on the slopes above. It didn't look good. There was an accumulation of soft snow before I dug down to hard climbable névé below. The soft layer could easily slide off over the harder layer as a massive avalanche.

Suddenly I heard a voice behind me. It was in English with a German-sounding accent, but it wasn't Karen. It was a man's voice. Was I hearing things? I turned around and there silhouetted against the light was one of the greatest Himalayan Climbers in history, the man who made the fast alpine style ascents on Hidden Peak in the Karakoram and the first ascent of Everest without oxygen with Reinhold Messner. It was Peter Habeler.

"Good morning," he said, "Ja, zee snow is no good, today we go down and tomorrow…?" He shrugged. We shook hands and he turned and was soon heading off down towards the fixed ropes and his girlfriend waiting in their camp below. I remember thinking how sad it was that these two superstar mountaineers, Peter Habeler and Reinhold Messner, who had been through so much together, had fallen out and were no longer friends.

Back at our camp, Karen made a brew and as we drank it struck me that at our much more modest level of mountaineering there was a slight parallel with Joe and me. We had been through a lot together and I certainly didn't want us to fall out. On the way down the fixed ropes Karen decided that as she still wasn't feeling too well and as she had limited holiday time left and had to be back at work, she would leave and head home. I decided to join her. For me one slightly intuitive interpretation of the whole season was that there was a series of signs telling me that things were not right. I had ignored most of them and carried on in the hope that things would come right on the mountain. It seemed about the right time to stop doing that before anything worse happened.

Joe and Ray eventually ground to a halt on their route at about mid height. Tony, Bruce and Ric climbed the face and turned around below the summit. Steve Hartland, despite being ill at the beginning of the trip, safely climbed to the summit and back.

Let My People Go Surfing, Yvon Chouinard, Yvon Chouinard Books, 2006

** *The Trekking Peaks of Nepal*, Bill O'Connor

*** See *I'll Call You in Kathmandu*, Bernadette Mc Donald, published The Mountaineers, 2005

Where it all began: The Moon Inn, Stoney Middleton.

Our porters setting off from Pulga. Note the rifle. *(Courtesy of Rod Pawsey)*

First Kulu summit. *(Courtesy of Rod Pawsey)*

Richard Haszko negotiating the leech infest paddy fields on the way to Tent Peak.

Fancy Dress at Tupopdan Base Camp. Joe Simpson, John Stevenson and Andy Cave.

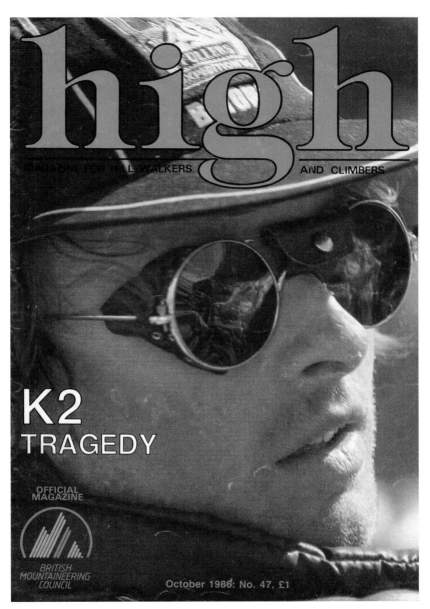

high

MAGAZINE FOR HILL WALKERS AND CLIMBERS

K2
TRAGEDY

OFFICIAL MAGAZINE

BRITISH MOUNTAINEERING COUNCIL

October 1986: No. 47, £1

My friend and mentor Al Rouse. *(Courtesy of Greenshires Publishing)*

The memorial to Ari Gunnarson that I made at Pumori Base Camp 2.

Steve Hartland on Pumori.

An OTT group on Island Peak with Phanden and Lakpa Gelu, 1999.

With Babu on Lobuche East.

131

Looking down to ABC on Cho Oyu.

Lhotse from the Khumba Icefall.

G2 from Base Camp.

A steep section near Camp 3 with
G1 behind.

A KE group returns safely from the summit of Khuiten in Mongolia.

Camp 2.

With Mick Bromley on Everest North Ridge. *(Courtesy of Stuart Holmes)*

Chapter 7

OTT Days

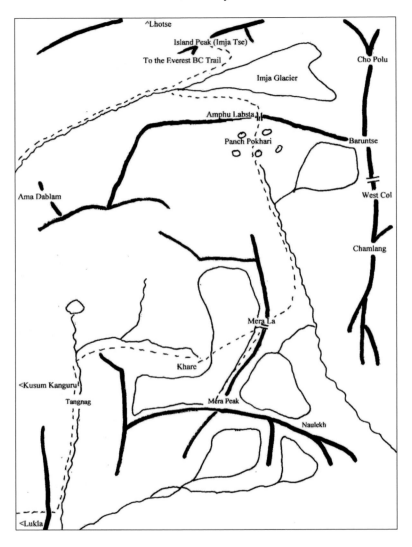

Map of Mera and Island Peak, Nepal

In my imagination I can see Andy Broome and Mark Miller sitting down together trying to brainstorm ideas for what they are going to call the new company that they have agreed to set up together. Ideas are rejected as being too dull or too pretentious and others for being both true and unlikely to attract any customers. Finally, as the afternoon is drawing to a close they hit upon Out There Trekking, a title with an inbuilt joke in that it would be referred to as being "OTT" (aka Over The Top). It was both sort of subversive and adventurous at the same time.

Looking back, the times that followed were certainly often OTT. Andy was the entrepreneur in the team as he already in the late 1980s and early 1990s had been organising and leading adventures and mountain travel to many wild places, including the then crumbling former Soviet Union. Mark was a strong and able climber and mountaineer and had spent the previous summers climbing new routes on obscure peaks in the Karakoram. Memorably for me, a few years earlier Al Rouse, with my belaying assistance, had in a good humoured way pipped him to the post in the race to make the first ascent of the route that eventually was entitled Rite of Way in the Wynnats Pass in the Peak District.

The HQ of their enterprise, Out There Trekking Ltd, was the tiny box bedroom of Mark and Cath's very modest terraced house in Sheffield. In October 1992, not long after OTT had been founded, Mark and his friend Victor Radvils boarded a flight from Pakistan where they had been climbing in the Karakoram to fly to Kathmandu for the autumn season in the mountains of Nepal. On board there was also a group from Plas Y Brenin who were aiming to climb Annapurna 1. They never made it. In low cloud, on the approach to Kathmandu, the plane flew straight into a hillside killing all passengers and crew.

So much was lost in that moment. There is a certain, if not expectation then at least consciousness of the likelihood that people can and do get killed in the mountains. It is somehow all the more shocking to be killed on an international flight between two major cities.

When he could finally come to grips with the shock and loss of his friend, Andy began to think about what to do. He invited Cath to join the company. At the time Cath was working in a managerial role in the Sheffield Education Department School Meals Service. She rang me as a former employee of the same local authority to talk it over. The prospect of adventure and the offer of a redundancy payment tipped the balance for her, I think.

I first met Andy with Cath sitting outside a lodge at the side of the airstrip at Lukla, the landing point for both treks and expeditions to Everest. I had been in the mountains for a while and probably looked a bit on the wild and woolly side. I was impressed by them though. They were sitting calmly in the sun waiting for their gear to arrive on another tiny plane from Kathmandu. Next to them they had a wine box and each had a glass of red wine. Andy offered me one. I liked him immediately!

Back in the UK Andy needed to try to solve a practical problem. He had to find someone who could fill the void left by Mark to lead some of the treks and climbing trips. He eventually asked Jon Tinker to join him. Jon, like Joe Simpson, was a great friend of Mal Duff's and had climbed a lot with Mal in Scotland and in the Himalaya/Karakoram. With the three of them OTT would both rise and fall.

For many people the landmark birthday of 40 can be a depressing one, a feeling of being if not OTT yourself, then perhaps past one's peak. Now, though, looking back many years, I can't see why anyone should feel that way. Even at the time I wanted to celebrate it rather than moan. I decided that in the year in which I was 40 I would climb 40 mountains. I would define my own rules about it. They all had to be over Munro height, that is 3000 feet (and many were indeed Munros), and they all had to be peaks that I had not climbed before. It was just a bit of fun but I thought I would do a bit of a charity fund-raiser along the way.

I didn't really have a plan. It never really registered that it was not far off one summit a week throughout the year. I knew though that work and the rest of life would determine where and when I could go. My loose, light-hearted aim for the year would draw me into both OTT and a new aspect to my life for many years.

Even before it began, there was a lot to contend with. My Dad, at 80, very much alone since Mum died in 1990 and with increasing dementia, died suddenly of a heart attack at home in November 1994. As with my Mum I was away in the Himalaya at the time, but my brother Rob got a message to me and I was able to get home in time for the funeral. Of course being at the funeral is less important than the quality of the relationship that we had for the previous 40 years, but it was obviously good to be there.

I'm sure that I didn't turn out as Dad had hoped. He, in an affectionate way, referred to me as the black sheep of the family. Then on the 7th of January 1995, after a long and terrible struggle with throat cancer, Janet's Dad died too.

On the 11th of January 1995 my year of climbing 40 peaks technically began. Then suddenly, and perhaps most shockingly, in March, Janet's sister - a lifelong sufferer from epilepsy - died from asphyxia in bed. She was in her mid-30s. Life seemed both very precious and very fragile indeed.

At the time Janet led the International Section within the School of Nursing and Midwifery at Sheffield University. She was involved in delivering a long term contract in Pakistan to improve the quality of Nurse Education in some key centres in the country. In the summer she went to Pakistan for several weeks. She worked mainly in Peshawar and Quetta and was welcomed into a quite different and delightful Pakistan from my own climbing experiences. There is a parallel world in Pakistan, the world of women. Today Quetta is one of the strongholds of the Taliban and almost certainly all the good work and enthusiasm has now, like so much else in the country, been wasted.

While she was away I had an idea. I called Andy at OTT and signed on as a client on a two-week trip to visit the Caucasus Mountains and Elbrus in Russia. Andy was leading the trip. Elbrus was not particularly interesting but trekking and climbing elsewhere was more like a real expedition. There were no porters, no lodges and the mountains, particularly the Bezingi Wall area, seemed much higher than their rather modest 4000m measurement.

Then, at the end of Janet's work trip I flew out to Pakistan to join her. The plan was to visit Chitral, the region of the country in which Tirich Mir (7750m) stands and where Pakistan borders with Afghanistan. We had planned to hire a driver and an air conditioned Pajero Land Cruiser to ease the discomfort of the arduous journey across the hot plains and up over the Lowari Pass. As we had been apart for several months, despite it being a Muslim country, I had also smuggled a bottle of Champagne in my luggage and we pictured a comfortable journey followed by sipping champagne on the lawns of our hotel with a view of Tirich Mir in the background.

Optimism is a good thing, but as could have been predicted the Pajero broke down terminally a couple of hours out from Islamabad and we had to hitch a ride in a local, grossly overcrowded mini bus. We arrived exhausted and covered in dust and mud in the middle of the night and found our hotel room awash with cockroaches. When we did get around to opening the Champagne some time later the heat, the bumpy roads and the altitude made most of it explode all over the floor. It was great to be there together though.

There was no time for a full climbing trip, but we did scramble up a rocky ridge to a small summit near a place famous for its hot springs called Garam Chasma. It was Peak 27 of my target 40.

On our return home from Pakistan we were met with some further shocking news. Paul Nunn, a friend from around the corner from our home in Sheffield, one of the few survivors of the generation of Al Rouse, Pete Boardman and many more, had been killed with his friend Geoff Tier as they descended from making the first ascent of Haramosh 2 in Pakistan. Paul had been my sponsor to join the Alpine Club and was also the President of the British Mountaineering Council (BMC). He was in his fifties, a university lecturer and had been on more expeditions than most people could imagine. Just minutes from the safety of their Base Camp, a serac or ice cliff high above them that had hung there for thousands of years dislodged and fell, killing both of them instantly.

Other deaths of that summer included Paul Williams, the climbing guide book writer, falling off Brown's Eliminate (a rock climb at Froggatt Edge that he had climbed many times before) and the sad demise of Alison Hargreaves when she was blown from the Shoulder below the summit of K2.

Including time in Nepal leading commercial trekking groups, after which I climbed a few small peaks with my friends Rahar and Nuru Sherpa, by the end of October I had a tally of 33 peaks under my belt.

Meanwhile, whilst on another visit to Pakistan, the British Council had asked Janet if she would like to apply to lead a similar but full time project in Bangladesh. She visited Dhaka, the capital, for an interview, to see what the place was like and check out the official bungalow where we might live. She was offered the job. It was a big deal. We would have to let our house, I would have to resign from the partnership of an organisation consultancy in which I worked. I would have to find work in Bangladesh and, in order to meet the then British Council qualification for spouse's flights, health care etc., we would need to be married. Also, perhaps of slightly less importance, Bangladesh is famously low level, flooded and flat so I could fail in my 40 Peak Quest. We went for it. Sometimes you just have to.

On the 9th November we hiked up four Munros in Perthshire and in the evening, by chance, after seeing a sign on a lamp post, met my friend Richard Haszko who was working for Chris Bonington as his driver and projectionist on a slide show tour. We went to the show and then, with Janet's Mum

Audrey and her dog, all spent a pleasant evening together. It was my Stag Night and Janet's Hen Night, for which Chris kindly picked up the bar bill. On the 10th of November we got married in Perth Registry Office.

Eleven days later we landed in Dhaka in Bangladesh where we lived for the following three years. I had climbed 37 peaks. I didn't like the feeling of unfinished business. As a part of the contract with the British Council, however, we had one flight back to the UK each year. So, on the 1st of January 1996 I flew back to the UK and on the 5th drove to Scotland and hiked up my last three peaks. The final one, in the dark, was Ben Vorlich on Loch Lomond side.

Back in Sheffield I was staying with our friends Pete and Gill. Together, they had bought my old house in Steade Rd, now converted from an unofficial open invitation international climbers' doss house into a modern home. They had invited several friends over for a small party to celebrate. I was very touched. On the 15th of January, now aged 41 I flew back to Dhaka. I was pleased.

Before leaving for Nepal for the Pumo Ri expedition with Joe, Andy Broom contacted me from OTT and asked if I would like to assist leading a group in Nepal over the winter. I thought it was a great compliment, but on reflection perhaps there are not all that many people who would be keen to lead a group of people that they have never met over three Himalayan summits during the winter, including both Christmas and New Year. I was.

Andy and Jon had come up with a complex scheme. They had 12 clients with varying abilities and ambitions and three guides, with Jon at the top of the hierarchy, then Seattlite Morris Kittleman, then the new boy, me. Various sub groups would turn back at various points along the way, mostly to get home by Christmas. I was to lead the hard core team for the full 29 day mission.

I was impressed. We appeared to have the best gear available, all the safety gear including a Gamow Bag, excellent food, but most importantly, working with us were some of the finest Sherpas I would ever meet. The Sirdar was the great Babu Chiri, with whom I would share many adventures over the next few years. Even then he was relatively famous, having climbed, amongst other things, Everest six times without oxygen. If he had been a European or American mountaineer he would be a regular on TV and in the newspapers and relatively wealthy too. To look at Babu, he did not strike you as a world class high altitude mountaineer. He was fairly short and stocky with a bit of a stomach and a big smile. Martin Brice, one of the group members and a journalist on the Financial Times, described him as a short man who was a giant amongst us.

I learned a lot from Babu, some very useful things about being in the mountains and others not quite so. One day, later on this first trip for example, he grabbed me by the arm and pointed skywards. "Tom Dhai," (literally meaning older brother), "see those clouds up there?" I peered up at the wind-streaked clouds sneaking over the nearby ridge. "When you see clouds like that the weather will change in four days," he paused and I nodded, absorbing the wisdom from the great guru ... "or it won't." He smiled and shrugged. "Thank you, Babu Bhai," (younger brother), I replied, "I will always remember that," and I have.

Our first objective was Mera Peak, an easy angled but high (6476m) and cold mountain that required a pass at over 4500m to be crossed and a high camp at 5800m to gain the summit. From Lukla airstrip it would take about ten days of trekking to reach it. These days, having climbed the mountain maybe twenty times, it is clear to me how things have changed. The beautiful and dense rhododendron forest above Lukla has been largely chopped down for firewood and the trail, previously with minimal signs of humanity and no permanent occupation, is now dotted with lodges.

In 1996 even the solitary hermit lama who lived under a rock near the only settlement Tangnag had given up and moved to a more comfortable location. The glacial lake above Tangnag was also still intact. In 1999 it burst its 100 metre high moraine walls and devastated with flood and millions of tons of rock not only the whole area but the agricultural plains many miles away and far below. Amazingly nobody was killed. The locals, ever wary, saw the moraine begin to break up and ran up the hillside to safety.

In December 1996 we were the only group on the mountain. After Mera we continued on into an even more remote valley, the Hongu, and trekked beneath the walls of Chamlang and Baruntse before tackling one of the finest pass crossings in Nepal, the Amphu Labsta. From a camp by a frozen lake we worked our way up a series of ice ledges and slopes using fixed lines that Babu and his team had rushed ahead to arrange to safeguard both the porters and ourselves. The top of the pass is about two feet wide with a drop of thousands of feet falling away in both directions. It is difficult to see how to get off. More fixed lines lead down to an even steeper rocky section. Here the team was carefully supervised down and then lowered by rope by Babu to join a long line of hundreds of metres of fixed ropes heading down towards the valley. Again supervision was essential here in case an error was made changing ropes at anchor points. I also kept the less confident clients short roped so I could hold a fall if necessary. At this stage brains can get addled with altitude, tiredness and fear and a slip would be fatal.

Eventually, late in the afternoon we arrived at the next camp, the turn-off point where many of the group would head back down to Kathmandu and eventually home for Christmas.

The rest of us, including Morris and Babu, would continue on to Island Peak. After Island Peak (officially called Imja Tse), Morris and some more of the team headed down and Babu and I were left with a small team of four, another peak to climb (Lobuche East), another pass to cross (the Cho La), a walk-up view point called Gokyo Ri and Christmas to contend with. It was all a delight.

The following spring Andy again asked me to lead a trip in Nepal for OTT. This time there was no hierarchy of guides, just me and the Sherpa Team. Of course it was a gesture of trust in me, but also a reflection of the fact that the most experienced leaders and sherpas, including Babu, were on another OTT expedition, this time to climb Cho Oyu from Tibet. Cho Oyu is the sixth highest mountain on earth and a mountain that would occupy much of my time and dreams in future years too.

The trip to the Rolwaling Himal went well except that we couldn't quite make the summit of either of the peaks due to poor weather and snow conditions. Although it is always disappointing not to reach the summit, a more realistic way of reflecting is I think to consider that if reaching the summit was inevitable, it would hardly be worth trying.

On the way down, having crossed the final difficult pass (the Teshi Labsta), we passed two other groups of trekkers on their way up in the other direction. The first told me that Tony Blair had just been elected as British Prime Minister and a Sherpa with the second group told me that the thought-to-be indestructible Mal Duff had died in the night in his tent at Base Camp whilst leading and Everest Expedition. In just a few minutes the world and how I understood it had changed in many different ways.

In general I like such encounters with other travellers. It is the way things have been for thousands of years in the mountains, passing on news about the trail, the weather or who you might meet ahead by word of mouth. It enriches the experience. These days the widespread use of satellite communications and so on has the opposite effect, it takes you out of the place and time. It impacts both judgement and safety and makes you depend on others, not on your own judgement. It can make you lose your concentration and make you homesick. Put perhaps too simply, if you think you can be rescued from anywhere, you are more likely to think that you need to be.

I only led one more trip for OTT over Christmas and that was to the volcanoes in Ecuador. It was memorable for a different reason, though. I had already climbed Cayambe and Cotopaxi once (nearly twice, except a blizzard kept us from the final summit) and then we moved on to Chimborazo. On the evening of Christmas day 2000 we arrived late at the Whymper Refuge (Edward Whymper famously made the first ascent of the Matterhorn in 1865 and then Chimborazo in 1880). By some measures Chimborazo is the highest mountain on earth as the summit, although only 6310m above sea level, is the furthest point from the centre of the earth as it is more or less on the equator. I cooked a makeshift sort of Christmas meal for the team and crashed out in my sleeping bag for a few hours' rest before yet another well-before-dawn, so-called "alpine start". The purpose of starting very early in the mountains is mostly safety. On many mountains, but on Chimborazo in particular, when the sun hits the higher slopes the risk of falling rock, ice and avalanches increases dramatically. The snow also turns to sugar, making every step hard work and dangerous.

There was one other group on the mountain, a guided group from a North American company. Our ascent went pretty smoothly. The route ascends steeply from the refuge to below a huge cliff. We nipped along "El Corredor" below it before the stones started coming. From there the route joins a glacier and takes a big zigzag first right and then left, leading to not far above the top of the cliff. We climbed the steeper section of the glacier in a few pitches of roped-up climbing, using ice screws as anchors on the steep terrain. The glacial bowl above was crevassed but straightforward and we carefully wound our way through the barrier that led again to steeper ground. The upper slopes require a peculiar effort to get through as they are made up of chest-high ice pinnacles called penetentes. These features are both rare in any mountains in the world and difficult to manoeuvre through.

The Veintemilla summit (6267m), once we had passed all the false summits, was as good summits should be and although not quite as high as the main Whymper Summit, a further hour away was good enough for us. We enjoyed it with plenty of hugs and handshakes, photographs and thoughts about future plans and so on.

It was on our way down that we caught up with the American group as they approached a crevasse at the top of the last more difficult pitch. One of them lost his footing on a snow bridge and fell into a crevasse, pulling all his team mates flat onto the ice. He was held by his team mates but had damaged, possibly broken his leg and couldn't move. Ossy (our local Ecuadorian Guide) and I rushed over to help, stepping over some of the other team, still pinned to the ice by the tension in the rope. It was immediately obvious to everyone that the accident had happened at the worst possible place. Immediately below us were the steepest sections of climbing. For some of the people it would be difficult enough with two good legs. What made things worse was the fact that if we didn't move quickly we would be passing under the famous rock fall area of El Corredor at the most dangerous time of day.

Both teams joined forces and, after a short discussion we decided that the only safe and fast way out was to tie two ropes together and lower everyone straight down. It would avoid the more difficult climbing which would be impossible for the injured climber and give people a chance to get past the rock fall danger. I took the frame pad out of my pack and we improvised a splint with this and straps and bandages and then we started lowering the two teams. It took the full length of two ropes to reach the bottom. I abseiled down and secured a place at the base. Eventually everyone reached me. From there we set off in three groups: Ossy and me with most of the clients and the American guide and his local guides helping their injured member hobble down. At times we had to fix ropes on tricky sections ahead of them and at others we could just walk or move together roped up.

When we thought it was nearly over and we would soon catch a glimpse of the refuge far below we were shocked to see and hear the deafening roar of hundreds of tons of rock pour down the cliffs just to our right. There was nowhere to hide. Some of the boulders were the size of cars and the ground shook beneath us. It seemed to originate from somewhere above near our route. We eventually reached the refuge at 6.30pm as it was getting dark again.

I worked for OTT several times a year from 1996 until 2001 and was privileged to lead a total of sixteen trips for them, including three on which Janet was a member, four expeditions to Cho Oyu and one to Gasherbrum 2 (both 8000m peaks). These 8000m peak expeditions and the lessons learned are described separately in later chapters. They were great days.

In the summer of 2001 OTT, having been renamed Alpine Mountaineering, suddenly and without warning went into liquidation. It was ordered by the company accountants and was an immediate legal instruction. According to them the company had run out of money. Many of us who were working for the company and had nothing to do with the events that caused it to happen did not get paid. In fact the only ones who financially benefited were as usual more accountants. It was a bit of a drag, but I didn't mind that much. I had really gained more from those years than money could measure.

The end was a sad story that had begun in 1999 and didn't finally conclude until 2006. In 1999 OTT organised an expedition to climb Everest from the Nepal side. Jon Tinker was the leader. In 2006 the Independent Newspaper reported what happened in the following way:

"Michael Matthews the 22 year old son of a property millionaire scaled the 29,000ft summit in 1999 after paying £22,000 to a specialist expedition company (OTT) based in Sheffield. He became separated from his guide in a 100mph blizzard during the descent from the peak and is believed to have fallen to his death. Mr Matthews's body was never found. The ascent made Michael Matthews the youngest Briton to have climbed Everest (at that time). His father David spent 6 years preparing a rare private prosecution for manslaughter against the guide, the leader, Jon Tinker and the supplier of the oxygen."

Jon had returned home early from the expedition due to sickness. In the end the judge said :

"If ever a criminal charge should be emphatically dismissed this is it....The prosecution case was based upon pure and wholly impermissible speculation".

It was a terrible tragedy and a painful subsequent saga for everyone involved. People will draw different conclusions about the events, but one thing from my whole climbing life and the OTT period in particular for me that is indisputable is that mountains are undoubtedly objectively dangerous places and no-one is immune from that danger.

Chapter 8

The Turquoise Goddess

Map of the Turquoise Goddess

Andy Broom got straight to the point as ever. "How do you fancy leading a trip to climb Cho Oyu from Tibet in the spring?" he asked. Cho Oyu is 8201m and the sixth highest mountain in the world. I had never even been to 7000m at that time. I felt a rush of anxiety and excitement and mumbled something in reply. It wasn't a rational response, but a meld of many and some contradictory emotions. He wasn't really asking me either, he knew what my reply would be, but rather he was offering me a fantastic opportunity. The job would involve a lot of hard work organising things both in Kathmandu before we left, travelling across Tibet and on the mountain. I would need to liaise with the authorities in Tibet to arrange yaks and work closely with our Nepalese Sherpa crew to ferry supplies and fix ropes and camps. I would also have to deal with any injuries or emergencies that occurred. It was a heavy responsibility. There was also the scary possibility that I might climb the mountain.

Some people might think that leading a commercial expedition made up of people who are not able to operate autonomously on a high dangerous mountain is an overwhelming responsibility. On the other hand to be able to possibly give someone one of the great experiences of their lives in relative safety is both a great gift and an honour. "Wow, fantastic brilliant," was what of course I meant to say.

Andy went on to explain that I would be co-leader with my friend Morris Kittleman from Seattle. Morris had already summited Cho Oyu a couple of years earlier with the legendary Babu.

Ours would be a non-guided, "Professionally Led" expedition. The distinction was an important one. A Guide has close personal responsibility for the client. He or she might short rope them on steep ground and would ensure their personal safety at every stage. A guide would be taking a client to a location where usually they would not be able to go without them. A Professionally Led expedition on the other hand set everything up and laid on the camps, logistics, fixed ropes etc for climbers who could, within the confines of those arrangements, climb the mountain themselves. It was just as well because we had twenty clients all signed up and just four climbing Sherpas, including twins Phanden and Rinzi Sherpa who would be on their first 8000m peak expedition.

Phanden and I had climbed together leading a group in 1997 on Mera Peak and had become immediate friends. When I met him, he was a strong young Sherpa who, although keen, friendly and likeable, spoke little English and had only been to school for a couple of years. Now, nearly fifteen years after our friendship began, both he and his wife Sonam speak fluent English, their children are doing well at a private school in Kathmandu, they own a successful Trekkers' Lodge on the Everest Trail and Phanden, amongst many other things, has climbed Everest six times from both the north and south and runs a trekking and mountaineering company called Sherpa Climbing. Rinzi, his twin brother, now works as a Glacier Guide in the Mount Cook area of New Zealand. Mountaineering on big mountains is not a pastime for Sherpas, it can be the key to a better life.

The name Cho Oyu is generally thought to mean the Turquoise Goddess. In the Tibetan language, the word Chomo means Goddess and Yu is the colour turquoise, so today's spelling is perhaps only a slight corruption of this. The north facing side of the mountain, in Tibet, is mostly snow and ice and certainly can glow blue/green in the afternoon sunlight. Turquoise is also a favourite and much valued stone by the Tibetan people and used a lot in their jewellery. It is an attractive explanation and my preferred option. Apparently Heinrich Harrer, of the book and film *Seven Years in Tibet* fame, claimed that a lama (monk) had told him that it meant Bald Goddess, which just doesn't have such a romantic sound to it. Mr Harrer was undoubtedly a brilliant climber but I take much of his account and explanation of many things, including allegedly being only a reluctant Nazi and his claimed personal closeness with the Dalai Lama, with a pinch of salt, so personally go with the Turquoise rather than Bald Goddess option.

There are some people who are either in the very small group of elite high altitude mountaineers or the much wider population of people who have never been to an 8000m peak, who claim that Cho Oyu, the Turquoise Goddess is an easy 8000er. For the few people in the former group, the world's elite high altitude mountaineers, compared with, say, the Magic Line on K2 they may be relatively correct. For everyone else, there is no such thing as an easy 8000m peak.

In 1952 a team led by the legendary mountaineer Eric Shipton and including Edmund Hillary, George Lowe and others who would be on the 1953 Everest ascent, failed to climb the ice wall at 6800m on what is now known as the "Normal" or "Classic" Route. Since then many, many people have failed to reach the summit and others who perhaps started out thinking that it was an easy 8000m peak have died trying.

The summit was finally reached for the first time in 1954. It was achieved by a small informal group nominally led by Herbert Tichy with two other Austrian and seven Nepali Sherpa friends. They had minimal equipment, had oxygen only for a medical emergency and relied on each other as only friends can.

The informal organisation did not mean they lacked drive or focus. A Swiss team, some of whose members in 1952 had pretty much climbed Everest by climbing beyond the South Col, unlocking the route for the British the following year, were in hot pursuit and only a day or so behind them. Tichy and his friends climbed nearly 1300m from their highest camp to the summit, fully committing themselves and climbing on unknown terrain. They made it up and back safely, but as luck in the mountains sometimes goes, the weather closed in and the strong and experienced Swiss team following them a day or so later had to turn back.

For me it is that aspect of mountaineering that makes it so engaging. As I have said before, if reaching the summit was inevitable, it would hardly be worth going. It is all about the struggle and the style in which you try to get there rather than just being there. Personally I am usually very jittery on summits and am never keen to hang about any longer than is absolutely necessary. On every mountain, the summit is only halfway and the second half is often where things go wrong.

Many people might consider that climbing any mountains is a both pointless and unjustifiably dangerous activity. They quite probably are right, for that is its essential appeal. It is not about being in any way reckless though. At its best it is about discovering and steering along the line that divides life-enhancing adventure from life-destroying misadventure. The debate about different climbing styles, their underpinning philosophy and value is all a part of it. Quite clearly if you have climbed a big mountain by a previously unclimbed route in a team of two without pre-fixed camps and ropes, the achievement is rather different from following up a line of ropes and tents that someone else has established along a route followed by hundreds, maybe thousands of others. It is not that I think one or other is wrong, it is just important to appreciate that if you do the second style it is not the same as the first.

I have read criticisms of contemporary commercial expeditions by mountaineers of previous eras and certainly armchair mountaineers enjoy nothing better than to debate such things, but the world was different in earlier decades and it still is when you are out there. I believe that if, for example, Chris Bonington or Doug Scott were keen young alpinists in their twenties today, they would probably be working on commercial expeditions to high mountains as well as doing their own cutting edge adventures.

In the end, Phanden along with other Sherpas made his first ascent of the mountain in support of two particular clients, both strong and able mountaineers, who together I thought created a symbol of hope in a troubled world. Under the new, energetic and optimistic Labour Government that had come to power the previous year in the UK, The Good Friday Agreement had only recently been put in place bringing to a close decades of conflict in Northern Ireland. Gavin Bates from Northern Ireland and Pat Falvey from Eire went to the summit together. I don't think that it was intentional, but I liked the idea of it. A total of six clients summited and a further two reached the edge of the plateau at 8000m before turning back due to the cold.

Gavin however nearly didn't make it beyond Advanced Base Camp, let alone to the summit. When we arrived it was still knee deep in snow. A lot of spade work was required to clear the area and get the tents pitched. It was a busy place too. Many dozens of large, shaggy, horned yaks carried loads for each of the dozen or so expeditions on the mountain. The herders steered each convoy by shouting and throwing stones at the lead animals and those that wandered off to keep them on track. Once they reached the Camp they had to coax them to a halt and unload them. The yaks clearly wanted to be rid of their burdens but they are skittish and unused to carrying loads and, due to their large horns, dangerous at the best of times. Gavin and I were carefully making our way along one of the tracks in the snow near our tents when a yak, newly freed of its luggage, charged away from its attendant herder, head down, and horns pointing forward. I dived out of the way but the yak caught Gavin straight in the chest and pinned him to the ground, chest to forehead. Fortunately Gavin fitted almost exactly between the horns. In a remarkably cool voice, given the circumstances, Gavin requested that I should do what I could to detach the snorting, yet rather surprised beast from him. Clearly all three of us wanted the incident ended as soon as possible and after some negotiations we parted company without serious injury. I'm not sure who was the most shocked, it all happened so quickly: Gavin, me or the yak?

On the mountain I had never really allowed myself many summit thoughts. At the beginning of the expedition I was somewhat weakened by a chest infection, but was also largely occupied sorting things out low down on the mountain. Morris was particularly keen to get his friend Dave Shensted, one of the clients, up the mountain, but he only reached Camp 2 before the dreaded chest infection laid him out. Towards the end of the trip, fully recovered, I surprised myself by how well I seemed to be going. I climbed up to Camp 2 and on to 7500m twice, and spent several nights there and assisted with moving

Camp 3 to a better location. Even if there had been time for me to make a summit attempt, so lacking in confidence had I been that I did not have the essential goose down insulated suit or high altitude boots with which to do it. Conditions get drastically colder above 7500m. Nonetheless, I was pleased to have been going well at a new personal altitude record and thought that was that. Job done.

I was wrong. Back home I soon received an email from Andy Broom. How about leading another expedition to Cho Oyu ...this autumn, it said. It was almost beyond my comprehension. As a lad I had read books in which the very best climbers might go on an expedition to a big mountain as the culmination of a long mountaineering career, and now here I was, just an enthusiast who by an amazing stroke of good fortune was about to go on my second 8000m expedition in 6 months. "Great," I replied.

Although Cho Oyu can be seen easily from both the north (Tibetan) and south (Nepalese) sides, it is in fact a very isolated mountain. To climb on the Tibet side from Nepal requires about five to six days of driving and acclimatising to reach the small dusty settlement of Tingri. An off-road drive in a truck or land cruiser takes you to what is known as the Chinese Base Camp. The representative of the Chinese/Tibet Mountaineering Association will then arrange your pre-ordered and paid for yaks to carry all the supplies and equipment to the Advanced Base camp. Each expedition might need to ferry up to 60 yak loads of equipment and supplies up to Advanced Base Camp. The yak herders and of course the yaks can make the trek from the Chinese Base Camp to the Advanced Base Camp in a day, but the distance and height gain is too much for most foreign climbers so a midway camp has to be established on the moraines of the Gyabrag Lho Glacier.

Despite its remoteness and altitude, there is quite often

a heavy military presence in this area. The glacier leads to a historic crossing place, the snow covered Nangpa La. One of the few pass routes into Nepal, it is an ancient trade route and people still use it, driving their yaks over the snow and ice in all weathers carrying goods to sell in Namche Bazaar (many days' walk away on the other side). Yak skeletons are reminders that both these hardy animals and people get caught out and die there. Nonetheless, I have seen a yak with a brand new washing machine (still in its cardboard packing) being hauled over the pass. Those who are oppressed by the authorities in Tibet also use it as a means of escape and are sometimes shot at or scared off with gunfire.

Even from Advanced Base Camp it is still a long way to the summit. Altogether there are three Camps on the mountain with the main technical difficulties being an ice cliff below Camp 2 (the one that turned back Ed Hillary and company in 1952) and a rock band above Camp 3 that has to be tackled both on the way up and down on summit day. The summit itself is at the far end of a gently sloping plateau, all above 8000m. Unlike on smaller mountains you cannot just start at the bottom and climb to the top. Acclimatisation is needed and camps have to be set up and stocked.

From a particular camp you would first make a day trip up towards the next, returning to your original camp to sleep. The following day you might reach the higher camp and leave food, gas or equipment and again descend to sleep. On your third excursion you might spend the night at the higher Camp. On Cho Oyu most climbers would have spent a few nights at Camp 1 (6000m) and a night or two at Camp 2 before descending back to Advanced Base Camp to rest (which is still very high at 5700m approximately) before making a summit bid from Camp 3. All this of this is, our course, weather, health and strength permitting. Climbing a big mountain for most people is mostly a lot of hard graft.

The autumn 1998 OTT Cho Oyu Expedition was a multi-part plan that would involve not one, but two separate expeditions on the mountain. The "A" Team was to be led by Jon Tinker with several of the best OTT guides (including Nick Kekus) and the best Sherpas in the business including Babu Chhiri and Lhakpa Gelu (who claimed the speed ascent of Everest from Base Camp to the summit in a literally breathtaking 10 hours, 56 minutes and 46 seconds) and the best cook Da Tenzi. They would have a separate kitchen tent, dining tent and toilet, near to but separate from us, the "B" Team.

The A Team also had just one client, a Mr X. We were not told his name, just that we would know him as Cos. It was all very intriguing. Apparently Jon and Nick had already guided their secret client up Denali (Mount McKinley) in Alaska and the plan was that if all went well after Cho Oyu in autumn 1998 they were on for Everest in spring 1999. It turned out that the mystery Cos was an extremely nice chap. The camouflage of his identity was because he wanted to travel anonymously as he was a member of the Greek Royal family and was wealthy to the extent that he owned several (I forget how many) oil tankers amongst other things. He was open, friendly and amusing. Other than being royalty and owning oil tankers, he was just a regular sort of a guy. I liked him.

As plans go the first part of the one for spring 1998 nearly matched the reality. Jon, Nick, Babu and Lhakpa Gelu did get Cos to the top of Cho Oyu on 24th September. In fact he was going well. Unfortunately near the summit, Jon, who had previously climbed Cho Oyu as well as Shishapangma (both without oxygen) and was the first confirmed Englishman to climb the North Ridge of Everest, was not. Usually very strong he struggled, nearly collapsed and had to be assisted by the others and with bottled oxygen at Camp 3. By the time I saw him back down below Camp 1 at 64000m the following day he had recovered somewhat and dismissed the incident as something minor. It sounded to me (and I'm sure to the others around) like a classic case of a cerebral oedema (pressure on the brain that is caused by fluid accumulation), a life-threatening condition brought on by altitude and one which often, once experienced, seems to reoccur. Jon was not a man to openly discuss his feelings, but it must have been just as obvious to him. The safest course of action was an obvious but difficult one. Not to go to high altitude again. If he took it, it would of course not only drastically change his working life, but perhaps even more significantly impact his self identity. He was up to that point a successful high altitude mountaineer. On the other hand it might save his life.

The "B" Team, who were for self esteem reasons not to be referred to as the "B" Team, were, as in the spring, also not to be guided in the traditional sense, but again Professionally Led. I would be co-leader with Damian Benegas. Damian is one of twins otherwise known in the mountaineering world as the Patagonian Brothers. Born in Patagonian Argentina but resident in the USA, both Damian and his brother Willie are very strong both on technical rock and ice and in high mountains, although Damian had not at that time climbed Cho Oyu or any other 8000m mountain. For the summit the "B" Team decided to split into two with me leading the first summit attempt on 28th September from Camp 3. My little team was struggling with the altitude when we reached the Camp. It was bitterly cold and the snow was soft and deep. The following day, in the dark of the early hours of the morning, it took us a long time to climb the rock band above it even though there was a fixed rope to help.

Having helped the others, I climbed up last. Despite wearing my down jacket I was really cold. My feet were cold up to my thighs. I had never experienced cold like it. It wasn't just the actual temperature that caused it but the altitude. We were climbing, like most people at this altitude, without the encumbrance of bottled oxygen, but we were moving too slowly to warm up. I soon realised that to plod on mindlessly was likely to cause some serious cold damage to my feet. I needed to do something. We would be up above 7900m for several hours and I would certainly pay the price for it. I looked ahead at the sky above the summit plateau. Clouds were skating across. It was obviously windy and the prospects were not looking good. Selfishness made me want the weather to break, but guilt and shame stopped me saying anything. I called out to Babu and the other Sherpas that I had to descend. Babu replied saying that the weather was not good anyway.

I descended down the slope and abseiled off the rock band. No sooner had I got into the tent and taken my boots off to start to warm my feet than I heard a rattling noise. The others were back too. The weather was deteriorating and even the great Babu wasn't taking any chances. The group also seemed exhausted. Psychology plays a big part here. Had the conditions been right and we had all gone to the summit, everyone would have been elated. It was also clear that one member, Brian, was in some trouble. We put him on the oxygen supply and gave him various medications that we had in camp and immediately set about preparing fluids for him to drink. He came round a bit but there was no way that we could get him to a lower and safer altitude until the next day. Our plan had been that after the summit we would bypass Camp 3 and go down to Camp 2, allowing Damian and his group to spend the night at Camp 3 and have their go at the summit the following morning.

The weather continued to deteriorate but as planned in the late afternoon Damian and his sub team duly arrived. It was going to be a squeeze. Brian was safe and reasonably comfortable in his tent with another member of the group keeping an eye on him. We thought that the situation was relatively under control. That was until he needed to go to the toilet and he needed to go in a way that could not be accommodated using a pee bottle. We had little choice. We had to put Brian's boots on for him (he was already wearing his down suit) and, whilst carefully holding the oxygen bottle and mask, escorted him to a pre-dug scoop in the steep snowfield outside. We held on to him and helped him to do his business. High altitude down-filled suits have various zips and flaps built into them to accommodate these circumstances, so thankfully he didn't need to fully undress in the wind and snow.

The procedure however went badly insofar as he went inside his down suit rather than into the hole in the snow we had dug. He had to sleep in it nonetheless!

That night the storm raged and it was obvious that even if we had not needed all hands to help Brian down, there would be no summit attempt for Damian's sub group. We did all get down safely.

Back at Advanced Base Camp Brian was much recovered and came to my tent. He really appreciated all the efforts that had been made to look after him and acknowledged that what he thought was appropriate experience on Kilimanjaro and then Aconcagua was a quite different world from an 8000m peak in Tibet in September. He said that he had finished with mountaineering and gave me his ice axe and harness which I gladly accepted. He offered me the down suit too, but I politely declined!

I wrote in my diary, "A good trip that we ran well. Just bad luck with the summit." I then wrote a footnote: "One member of an American guided group died of exhaustion in his tent at Camp 2."

We had made some good decisions.

From 1995 until the autumn of 1998 Janet and I lived in Dhaka in Bangladesh. She was leading a British Council project working in collaboration with the Bangladesh Government to raise the professional status and skills of nursing in the country. Between trips I had been working as a consultant for UNICEF. It had been, as they say, a developmental experience, but one in which the longer ago it is, the more fondly and positively we recall it. I reckon that many people feel the same way about their experiences on 8000m peaks.

Soon after we returned to our home in Sheffield and had got ourselves sorted out, the phone rang. It was Andy Broom. So, like a glutton for punishment, in April 1999 I found myself back in Kathmandu organising my third expedition to Cho Oyu from Tibet.

Although the definition of what is meant by a Professionally Led expedition was clearly laid out in all the particulars to clients, I tend to think that many of them just looked at the price tag and saw that it was less than other companies were asking (for a guided trip). Also, being open to all comers certainly can make a strange group dynamic.

Sometimes I have been asked what type of people would join a commercial expedition. The answer is that they are from a wide range of countries, walks of life and ages. Perhaps 10-20% are women. As a broad generalisation I might expect to see clients of four different types. They might be quite competent mountaineers who for convenience and cost reasons just want to buy into the infrastructure but are quite capable of climbing themselves. The second type would be people who have done a lot of commercial climbing trips. They have a fantastic breadth of experience having possibly climbed all over the world, but because they have always been guided and have done little on their own, they might lack the depth of experience or confidence to do their own thing. People in the third group realistically know that they stand little chance of reaching the summit but really enjoy the whole experience of being on the trip. Those in a small final group have either deluded themselves or others into thinking that they are up to it.

In spring 1999 I had a sub-group of Chilean mountaineers, mainly women who wanted to make the first Chilean ascent of Cho Oyu. I also had police officers, a civil servant, a magazine publisher, scientists and a doctor. The doctor, who was much to my initial relief to take on the role of expedition doctor, unfortunately only made it to the Chinese Base Camp before he had to return home sick. Pollard and Murdoch* identify altitude anxiety as a genuine trigger for altitude illness. The widely noticed increase in the phenomenon probably correlates with the availability of information in books, magazines and on websites that people can read and worry about. It is almost as if by keeping running the message in your head that you must not get altitude sickness, your brain only hears the last three words and obeys. Perhaps a better mantra is "Keep well, keep strong", or just to mellow out a bit.

The mountain was quite crowded with, among others, a large Russian team, an American Women's team and several other big commercial groups. For me, far from being hostile it had become a friendly place. I knew many of the other guides and would bump into mountaineers whom I had met or climbed alongside from many parts of the world. It was also great to be working again with many old Sherpa friends and to get to know the Sherpas from other expeditions. As well as my friend Phanden, another Sherpa friend, Pemba Gylgen, with whom I had worked on smaller mountains, was on his first 8000m trip.

It didn't all go smoothly though. Two further members of my group elected to return to Kathmandu with illness. On 7th May I had to escort another down from Camp 1, a very strong young Swedish adventurer who, having forced himself to reach Camp 1, was so exhausted he refused to look after himself and eat and drink. If I hadn't taken him down the deterioration would have just continued on its rapid inevitable course. On the same day, back at Advanced Base Camp, I heard on our walkie-talkie that a Spanish/Basque Guide had surprisingly early in the season taken a client to the summit. On their descent in the fading light they had failed to find the way down the rock band. The client had disappeared, presumably having fallen to his death and the guide was on the radio asking for help. He was above the rock band, beyond Camp 3 and it was nearly night time.

By an amazing bit of good fortune members of our Sherpa team had just arrived at Camp 2 that afternoon carrying full loads of tents and equipment. Without hesitation they set off again. They reached Camp 3 and climbed onwards in the dark. Pemba Gylgen, breaking his own altitude record, was in the lead. We were talking in radio contact throughout. Soon Pemba had climbed the rock band and was trying to locate the stranded Guide, who was getting more and more agitated in his radio communications. Eventually he was found and Pemba and the others helped him down. Back at ABC everyone hailed our Sherpas as heroes and the guide, in front of a big appreciative crowd, promised to give them $1000 as a thank you gift.

On the 9th of May Russell Brice and his team were heading towards Camp 3. Russell, one of the greatest mountaineers of our time and the most professional expedition organiser, noticed an unfamiliar shape in one of the gullies below the rock band, off route to one side. They climbed up towards the shape and found the lost client. He had been lying injured and exposed on the open snow slope for two days and nights. He had lost his gloves and was in a very bad way.

For the rest of the day about half the groups from many countries in Advanced Base Camp rallied around to help carry him down. He was on an improvised stretcher and breathing bottled oxygen. At Camp he was rested and rehydrated and then had to be carried on the back of a yak down to Chinese

Base Camp, then on to the road and driven to Kathmandu for medical treatment. In the end I understood that he lost some fingers to frostbite, but was able to return to his job at a bank.

When we came to packing up the Advanced Base Camp at the end of the expedition, I went to the Spanish/Basque camp and reminded the guide about his promise of a payment to the Sherpas. He assured me that he would sort it out in the morning before he left.

The next morning I caught him before he left and took him to our kitchen tent where the Sherpas were waiting. He tried to deny making the promise, but wisely realising that he was rather outnumbered grudgingly paid over the money, accusing the Sherpas of being greedy and dishonest. Rubbish, of course, and without them he would have been dead.

By the end only four of the OTT clients were up to making a summit attempt. Pemba Gylgen, the hero of the moment, made it with two of the Chilean women. I subsequently reached the rock band with friends Graham Illing and Nick Burring but the snow conditions were poor and the weather was against us. I thought that I was never going to get up this mountain.

During the same season, round in Nepal on Everest, Babu Chhiri made his ninth ascent of Everest and spent the night alone in his tent on the summit, a record that has never even been attempted since. In October Tat died in a paragliding accident in Greece.

On my fourth and (probably) last trip to Cho Oyu in the autumn of 2000 I hoped things would go well. I had an early problem with one client with whom (having seen her very attractive photograph and read her quite appropriate resumé in Kathmandu) I was impressed. When I met her I immediately realised that neither matched up at all to the reality. It was obvious that she was completely out of her depth, not experienced in the way the resumé indicated, ill equipped and ill prepared even when she struggled in to Advanced Base Camp. For her own safety I allocated a Sherpa to be with her all the time beyond this Camp.

Towards the end of the expedition on the 21st September, when the rest of the group were ready to make their summit bids or had given up, she had just reached Camp 1 for the first time. I decided that Camp 1 would be her high point and that we needed the Sherpa to help with the rest of the group, so told her that she must go down and that I would escort her back to Advanced Base Camp.

To say that she was cross would be to understate it. She had a tantrum of swearing, shouting and throwing things about. It was a bit scary, but merely reinforced the correctness of my decision. One of the clients, Hamish Fulton, and one of our kitchen staff volunteered to help and we descended together for a while from Camp 1. Later the two of us negotiated the crevasses on the glacier and walked along the moraines to Advanced Base Camp. I was subjected throughout to a constant stream of verbal abuse and hatred, declarations that nobody, including her mother, her boyfriend and the other guy she was seeing loved her and various suggestions that she should throw herself in a crevasse. Eventually I radioed in advance to Camp and some of the crew came out to help escort her back. I returned back up to Camp 1. By the time we got down from the mountain she had left for home with another group.

Although again technically this was not a guided trip, it finished up being a bit that way. The summit day was busy with many people heading in the same direction. I was climbing with Hamish Fulton, who in his other life is a renowned modern artist. We were going slowly, but as we approached the summit plateau I remember getting an overwhelming feeling that nothing

169

could stop us. I was feeling strong, the weather was good and the snow conditions underfoot were fine.

Clients and husband-and-wife couple Mauricio and Badia Lopez went past on their way to make the first Mexican ascent of the mountain. Russell Brice moved past leading his clients, several of whom were using bottled oxygen. Another of his clients, the charming Marcos Siffredi, more or less ran past on his way to snowboard from the summit. American climbing legend Charlie Fowler moved past cracking a joke and with a word of encouragement. Finally Sherpa friends Phanden, Pemba and Ningma went by, first checking that we were okay. Behind us, climbing in our trail, was American climber and skier Laura Bakos, towing her skis and aiming to make the first female descent of the mountain. It was a great atmosphere.

Suddenly the angle of the terrain changed. We were on the summit plateau. I could see the people on it. We moved along for a while and I could even hear their voices. Fantastic. I had however been completely in my own zone. I turned and looked at Hamish. We were over 8000m. He looked rough. His speech was slurred and he was a bit disorientated. I looked at the summit and saw Russell Brice approaching. He looked at Hamish too and I said that I thought it was as far as we should go. To get there and back to this spot would take the best part of an hour and a lot can happen in that time. "Well done," Russell said and began his descent. Hamish took some photographs and we began to descend too.

At the rock step I checked that Hamish was safely and correctly attached to the abseil rope and sent him down first. He disappeared over the edge and I expected him to be off the rope in a minute or two and that after I rejoined him we would soon be heading for Camp 2. I felt the rope, it was still weighted. I called out and got no reply. After a while I secured myself and peered over the edge. It was hard to make out what was going on, all

I could see was the top of his hat and him slumped against the rope. He still didn't respond. I feared the worst. Fortunately there was a second rope nearby so I abseiled down on it to see what I could do.

Hamish had got his abseil device tangled and locked in the rope. Dangling from a rope alongside him it took me quite a while to safely get him to unload his weight long enough to free the device. We were still well over 7600m. Eventually we were free and abseiled down the remaining rope.

The plan had been to descend all the way to Camp 2 but that didn't by now seem feasible. My friend Henry Todd kindly offered to squeeze us into his already overcrowded tents. Hamish and I were separated but he was not alone in a tent and I was sharing with seven others in a huge tent called a Himalaya Hotel.

The next morning while I was still enjoying some tea in my sleeping bag, Hamish appeared at the tent door. Immediately I was filled with fear and anxiety. We were camped on a very steep snow slope with a long drop all the way to Camp 2 and we were still at over 7500m. Hamish was only wearing his thermal inner boots on the snow, the soles of which are smooth and slippery, and he didn't have a hat, warm clothing or snow glasses on. I could just imagine a disaster. Fortunately it was averted and we did descend without further incident.

Some people say that it is impossible to guide other people at the highest altitudes and that really it is every man or woman for him/herself. All I can say is that from my experience up to that point, without using bottled oxygen I was able to make a decision of which I was proud. I may not have quite reached the summit, but I became a better mountaineer.

Mauricio and Badia Lopez did make the first Mexican

ascent and went on to Everest and Makalu in later years. Russell Brice, trading as Himalayan Experience, remains the top expedition outfit for 8000m peaks. Marcos Siffredi did snowboard from the summit and then went on to snowboard down the Norton Couloir on Everest, but sadly disappeared attempting to do the same on the Hornbein Couloir in 2002. Charlie Fowler disappeared in China with his partner, the extremely accomplished mountaineer and contender to be the first woman to climb all fourteen 8000m peaks, Christine Bostok, probably overwhelmed by an avalanche. With a bit of help from her friends, Laura Bakos became the first woman to ski down Cho Oyu.

Hamish went home to work on his exhibition at the Tate Modern in London.

The High Altitude Medicine Handbook, A.J. Pollard and D.R. Murdoc, <u>Radcliffe Medical Press</u> ,1997.

Chapter 9

All Change

All Change

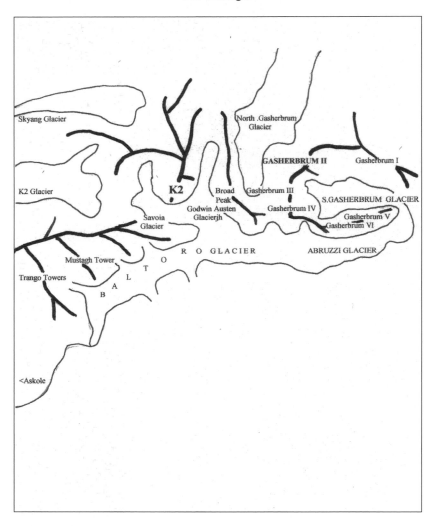

**Map of the Baltoro Glacier and Gasherbrum Group,
Pakistan**

There are times in our lives when things of cultural or historical significance happen and we can remember quite clearly where we were and what we were doing when we learned about them. When England won the World Cup, the shooting of John Lennon or the death of Princess Diana might be examples.

An early one for me was in 1977 when I was sitting outside my tent at the base of Mount Kenya. My friends were still on the mountain and I was brewing up on a small fire. In one direction was the mountain and in all the others was shimmering savannah grassland, blowing in the light breeze. On the horizon I noticed the silhouette of a man. He must have seen the smoke from my fire. He began moving towards me. I felt a bit uncomfortable. What did he want? At first he walked but then gradually he broke into a slow loping jog. As he got nearer I could see he was a tall local man. He carried a staff and was wearing traditional clothing. The jog seemed to be gaining a sense of urgency. Was he going to rob or attack me? I didn't really know what to do. I was a bit anxious, but there was nowhere to go so I just sat there.

Eventually he arrived at my camp, slightly breathless. He towered above me as I sat hunkered on the ground. He looked at my fire and my possessions strewn about. After a long moment, perhaps summing me up, he said...

"Do you know that Elvis Presley is dead?"

It was certainly not what I expected him to say, but he was right. Later I learned that Elvis had died that morning. It was the 16th August 1977.

We talked a bit more about Elvis and other musicians that we both enjoyed such as Jimi Hendrix and then moments later he was gone, disappearing into the grasslands once more, leaving me alone again to contemplate a world without Elvis.

The year 2001 had many of those days. You just don't forget them. So much changed. In January OTT Expeditions changed its name. After the tragic death of Michael Matthews, and the mystery Greek shipping magnate, known to us simply as Cos, reaching the summits of Denali and Cho Oyu, Cos also summited Everest on the spring 1999 trip. Sadly, on his return home to New York he too died. His death was thought to be exacerbated by a combination of a lifelong minor heart defect, his rapid return from altitude, long international flights and, allegedly, once home, the use of recreational drugs. Subsequently, Andy and Jon also parted company and Jon left the business. So, from January 2001 OTT became the renamed Alpine Mountaineering.

In February, after an excellent winter in the Scottish

mountains, I led the first Alpine Mountaineering trip to walk up Kilimanjaro in Tanzania. It was a pleasant outing made all the more so because Janet came along too. The prospects for the year ahead were, I thought, looking good, but I am an incurable optimist.

Back home, by the end of the month admittedly things didn't look quite so rosy. The hills and mountains of the entire UK were suddenly closed due to an outbreak of Foot and Mouth Disease. It was a disease which hadn't existed in the UK for decades. It generated a full-scale government and media panic. The countryside was closed, animals were slaughtered and incinerated, farmers were, it was said, over-generously compensated whilst many other businesses not eligible for compensation went to the wall. It was nobody's finest hour.

During the first few days of March Andy Broom and I had several telephone conversations. He had another small group for an Everest Expedition from the Nepal side booked, but the finances were tight. He needed someone to do the entire organisation and deal with the formalities and supervise the transport of all the food, equipment and supplies to Base Camp. In addition he had a trekking group in support of the climbing team who would visit Base Camp and climb Island Peak. Above Base Camp on the mountain Willie, Damian Benegas's twin brother and Scottish Mountain Guide Sandy Allen would lead the trip. It was suggested by Andy that rather than being paid for all of this he could put my name on the Everest Permit. It sounded like a great idea to me. I flew out to Kathmandu on 17th March to begin work.

Then as things progressed Andy suggested by email that I should perhaps be paid instead and then I would be able to concentrate on the job of establishing everything at Base Camp (It would also be much cheaper). Although a little disappointed I couldn't really complain. I would be paid and would be trekking in beautiful Nepal and meeting up with my Sherpa friends including Babu (by now running his own company, Nomad Expeditions), Phanden and Pemba Gylgen. Hopefully I would also be able to give the trekking and Island Peak party an adventure of a lifetime and set things up for a successful Everest climb. There were many worse things to be doing. Eventually, after several weeks of hard work, all the yak loads of supplies arrived at Base Camp. I followed and spent a night at the settlement of Lobuche (4900m) on my way to meet the main party at the Base Camp.

On the evening of 6th April, as I sat in the lodge in Lobuche drinking tea, I was soon thinking of other matters. My old friend of many OTT trips, Babu walked in. It was great to see him and we spent the evening sitting by the fire chatting and catching up on news of family and friends. We talked about our times together on Cho Oyu and on several smaller peaks, his ten times on the summit of Everest without bottled oxygen and his night alone in his tent overnight on the summit. He said that if the weather was fine and he felt good he might go to the summit again this season, but if not he would just rest. He was not driven by ambition. When we eventually parted company and headed for bed a young American trekker approached me. He asked me if the guy I was talking to was the great Babu Chhiri. I said he was. He said that he would have loved to have talked to him but felt embarrassed butting in on a conversation with the great man. Had he known, Babu would have been embarrassed himself about being held in such awe. He was still the modest, unassuming and straightforward family man from the village of Taksindu in the Khumbu, but he was becoming justifiably famous.

The next day I headed off early up to Base Camp to join our Sherpas and the client group for a puja. A puja is a traditional blessing that takes place before every expedition in Nepal. A lama or monk chants some prayers, prayer flags are flown, incense is burned and rice is thrown in the air. Nobody ever ventures onto a mountain before the puja.

I spent one night at the Base Camp before heading back down to Kathmandu to clear the imported supply of Russian-made oxygen bottles through customs and to arrange their transport to the mountain for use towards the end of the expedition. Babu arrived as I was leaving and we had a brief chat before I set off. That was the last time I ever saw him. By the 29th April the great Babu Chhiri was dead.

The story was that during the afternoon when he arrived at Camp 2 he was taking a photograph of his tent and fell backwards and headfirst into a hidden crevasse. He wasn't found until midnight. The next day Willie, Sandy and all the Sherpas managed to get his body out of the deep twisting hole in the ice. It took about a further eight hours for them to carry him down the Western Cwm and through the dangerous and difficult Khumbu icefall. A Nepalese Army helicopter took the body from Base Camp. A Nepalese national icon and hero was lost in that moment, but so was a husband and father of six daughters and a friend and inspiration to many. He is still sorely missed.

I returned home for just a month in the summer of that hectic year and then at the beginning of June I landed in Islamabad International Airport, Pakistan to lead an Alpine Mountaineering group on Gasherbrum 2 (8035m) in the Karakoram. Of the fourteen mountains in the world that are above 8000m, Gasherbrum 2 only just qualifies and is the "lowest" on the list.

Mounting any expedition in Pakistan is much more difficult than in Nepal. The bureaucracy is more problematic; the mountains are a long way from the cities so require domestic flights or long arduous road journeys, and they require long approach treks, all before you even start to climb them. The geology of the Karakoram also makes them steeper and rockier. There is good reason why, for example, unlike on Everest there are very few commercial groups on K2, the second highest mountain in the world.

Our journey would begin in Skardu - the famous staging point for expeditions to the Karakoram including K2. Skardu can be reached by plane from Islamabad, weather permitting, or more usually by a thirty hour drive up the dusty and dangerous Karakoram Highway. A day's jeep ride on dirt roads then leads to the hamlet of Askole. From there the trek up the Baltoro Glacier takes about a week and passes Great Trango Tower, K2 and Broad Peak and eventually it reaches the Gasherbrum Base Camp.

Before I could even begin to address the plan for Gasherbrum 2 however I picked up the newspaper in the hotel lobby, *The Nation*. It was Sunday 2nd June. There was a picture of the Nepalese Royal family on the front page. It caught my eye. I had been visiting Nepal frequently since 1985. I was shocked to read the headlines. Ten members of the Nepalese Royal Family, including the King and Queen, had been apparently gunned down by the Crown Prince over a dispute about whom he should marry. The Crown Prince allegedly also shot himself too and later died. I wrote in my diary at the time:

"There is much speculation about what really happened - rumours about all sorts of plots and political intrigues. There have been riots in the streets of Kathmandu. Probably the only winners from the saga and confusion will be the Maoists and then everyone will lose."

It turned out to be not a bad prediction. The country in many ways still has not recovered or moved on.

When I was able to turn my attention to Gasherbrum

2, that was also not without its problems. At the time, in order to climb in most parts of the Karakoram, you needed a Permit and a government appointed, so-called Liaison Officer or LO. The reality was that the LOs were usually just on a money making trip. They had to be paid according to a prescribed scale and issued with the same standard of climbing equipment and clothing as the rest of the team. Most Liaison Officers stayed at Base Camp and sold their equipment either after or sometimes before the trip. The rules stated that if they wanted they could be an equal part of the climbing team, irrespective of their ability. It turned out that our Liaison Officer was a senior officer in the Pakistan Air Force (although he had never flown a plane) and told me that he was an enthusiastic supporter of the recent actions of the Taliban in Afghanistan as "upholders of the true faith". Personally I didn't think this was a very good combination. He also wasn't interested in doing much "liaising" for or with us, but I think he just wanted to enhance his CV and add Gasherbrum 2's summit to it.

Veteran Himalayan expedition organiser Henry Todd was also sharing our Permit and Liaison Officer and had two clients to add to my team of four. By the time we all finally arrived at Base Camp on 18th June it was clear to me that at least one of my clients had completely underestimated what was involved in climbing an 8000m peak. He had even struggled with the trek up the Baltoro Glacier and one of the high altitude porters had carried his pack for several days. Later it turned out that two more of my four clients to a lesser degree had massively underestimated what they were taking on and/or overestimated their own abilities. A combination of the wording of the brochure perhaps, possibly selective reading and misplaced ambition were maybe the reasons. The Alpine Mountaineering brochure said that Gasherbrum 2 is one of the easiest 8000m peaks, which is obviously quite different from saying it is easy. In fact it is both steeper and technically harder than Cho Oyu, as I was to find out.

The route up the mountain from Base Camp can be divided into four distinct sections. The first is up the glacier which includes many crevasses and a section of icefall. Camp One is on the glacier. The South-West Spur or Ridge then leads almost directly from the Camp to the site of Camp 2 at 6700m. Although mostly of moderate angle, the lower part of the spur is threatened by a hanging glacier above. Working in collaboration with David Hamilton, the leader of the expedition from another UK based company (Jagged Globe), we placed fixed ropes up the ridge all the way to Camp 2. You certainly wouldn't want to fall off. It was an avalanche here that buried the entire Camp One of the first ascentionists on the Austrian Himalayan Society Expedition of 1956, led by Fritz Moravec. Henry Todd and his two clients caught the edge of a similar avalanche at the same place, but luckily escaped without injury.

From Camp 2 the climb steepens to reach a shoulder at 7150m and the site of Camp 3. Some parties go directly from this Camp to the summit and back in a long day. Others establish a slightly higher camp below the summit pyramid at 7600m or so. On the first ascent three climbers - Moravec, Larch and Willenpart - set off from Camp 3 climbing without bottled oxygen. They bivouacked in the open at about 7500m before pushing on to the summit in perfect weather the next day.

On our trip, after we had spent a night at Camp 2 we returned to Base for a rest before making our summit attempt. I told the LO that he could not go any further. My reasons were that he didn't carry any loads, didn't do any cooking or melting of snow to make drinks and, to be frank, wasn't exactly convivial company. As he was employed in a very hierarchical organisation, the Pakistan Air Force, I rather thought that he would accept the decision of the leader. I did not imagine that he would take revenge for his ambition being cut short.

All Change

I made a summit attempt from Camp 3 with the one remaining client, Andy, and our high altitude porter Khan. At about 7400m, after a tricky rocky section, Andy declared that he had cold feet and wished to descend. The mountains of the Karakoram in the summer are not particularly cold, unlike for example Cho Oyu in September. I was climbing in fleece and Gore-Tex clothing and never used my one piece down suit His feet may have been cold in a different way, which is also okay.

It was a slight, but only slight dilemma. Khan had been to Gasherbrum 2 several times, but despite being local he had never been to the summit. For a brief moment it crossed my mind that I could send Andy down the fixed ropes with Khan and I could push on for the summit and even tag along with another group. It was obviously a ridiculous and selfish idea. If anything happened to Andy, I would never forgive myself and Khan had earned the opportunity to make it to the summit. I escorted Andy back to Camp 3 and Khan tagged along with another group and did finally make it. The next day Khan, Andy and many other summiteers descended together back down the fixed ropes to Base Camp.

Meanwhile at Camp 3 Henry Todd had asked me if I would like to join him and his two clients John and Dave to make another summit attempt. I understood the code and appreciated the offer. They would like me to do a bit of trail breaking. Henry and his team were all using bottled oxygen. I made one good and one bad suggestion. The good one was that we should establish a higher camp from which to attempt the summit. My bad suggestion was that we should just take the inner tent of a North face VE 25 tent and all four of us should squeeze in for a short pre-summit night to save weight.

On the 11th July we all made it to the site of Camp 4 without incident. It was obviously an exposed location as all around were bits of broken tent pole and flapping shredded tent fabric anchored frozen into the ice. It felt a bit eerie. The scariest bit of remains was however a leg with a plastic boot and crampon attached protruding out of the solid ice below the tents. Nobody seemed to know the story of who it was or when they died. The body would have been impossible to hack out of solid ice and then get off the mountain. Even then it would have been impossible to transport it from the Baltoro to anywhere before it decomposed.

Above us the weather looked ominous too. High lenticular clouds raced over the summit. That night it snowed heavily. The inner tent alone was not snowproof and I was not popular. Next morning we set off in the dark for the summit with me breaking trail and the others following. We were traversing underneath the summit rock pyramid. The angle of the snow slope was not extreme, but was gentle enough to have accumulated a good cover of fresh snow. I reached the furthest point of the traverse where you turn to climb the final section to the summit. The snow was getting very dangerous. At every step I sank to shin- or knee-deep and a huge slab would be sent skating down the slope below. I stopped and dug a hole to have a look at the layers. Even by my headlight in the dark I could see it was clearly in a dangerous condition. By the time we had gone to the summit and back the sun would have been on the slope and made it even more so. I turned to discuss it with the others. They, wrapped in their oxygen masks and just following my steps, had not realised the danger, but when they looked they agreed. With just a few hundred metres to go we turned and headed back down.

A short time later the Chilean leader of an expedition to a neighbouring mountain, Gasherbrum 1, was killed in an avalanche on an equivalent slope to our own. I was relieved that my assessment and decision had probably kept us safe.

At Base Camp it was clear that the LO was assembling

as much evidence as he could to complain about me. As I normally would when we cleared the Base Camp, I went across the whole area on my hands and knees picking up every item of litter or detritus. Every morning on the walk out I treated nearly all the porters for minor ailments. When I chose to leave via a high pass called Gondoro La to save several days trekking, the LO complained bitterly, saying that the porters didn't want to go. I asked them: they were happy as they had to work fewer days for the same money.

Back in Rawalpindi I had to go for the customary debrief at the Ministry of Tourism. The LO produced his long list of the "crimes" I had committed. They included giving a porter an antacid tablet that was one month out of date and not supplying adequate equipment to the LO. Apparently his new Mountain Equipment sleeping bag, which was better than mine, and his North Face Gore-Tex jacket were inadequate. I was fined, or rather required to personally pay the LO, an additional $450. What a racket. Fortunately, whilst much else in Pakistan has over the ensuing years got far worse, at least the Permit and LO system has now improved a lot.

By the time I got home on 22nd July I was beginning to feel tired from the stresses and strains of leading and organising so many high altitude expeditions, let alone from the climbing. I was beginning to think that maybe I needed a bit of a change.

On 8th August Alpine Mountaineering, which had only been in business since January, then ceased trading. It was the middle of the season for climbing courses in the Alps and there were several groups out there. Because it was an AITO member all the clients were safely brought home, but none of the guides were paid. Some thought and made accusations that some sort of conspiracy or rip-off was going on. Andy and Cath were shocked and distraught. In my view the only such thing that could be considered a rip-off was that other accountants who were brought in to close the business took what money remained as their fee. It was another of those times when legal and right are different things. I had also not been paid for the Gasherbrum 2 expedition, but I took a different view to some of the others. Money is important, but not everything. I had led eighteen trips for OTT/Alpine Mountaineering and had a great time and learned a great deal. That was worth a lot.

I found myself defending Andy and Cath. They were, I think, heartbroken and confronting everyone was just too hard. In the end they lost out the most. They lost their business, their income and eventually their home. In my diary I wrote, "For me, it probably has merely brought forward the lifestyle change I needed."

In between all the mountaineering trips I had also continued in my original profession in Human Resource Consultancy. I applied for a full time permanent job as the Management Development Consultant to the Chief Executive of Nottingham City Council. I was invited to an interview and to make a presentation to a group of managers on the 10th September. The following day, while I was travelling as a passenger in a car back from a meeting near London, listening in horror and silence to the description of the bombing of the World Trade Centre Twin Towers in New York on the radio, my mobile phone rang. It was the Personnel Officer at Nottingham City Council. I had got the job.

Everything was changing.

Chapter 10

Karakoram Experience

In 1984, friends Tim Greening and Glenn Rowley, with the help of some local contacts they had met the year before whilst trekking, started the company Karakoram Experience. They led one of the very first commercial treks up the Baltoro Glacier to K2 and Concordia. In subsequent years they went on to lead and organise dozens of other groups on a variety of previously unknown trekking routes across the Karakoram. Many of these treks have now become established 'classics' and are described in guidebooks around the world.

I first encountered a Karakoram Experience (otherwise known as KE) group below Gondoro Peak in Pakistan in the summer of 1988. Over the following years I would meet up with them in the Khumbu and Annapurna areas of Nepal as well and would also became friends with their other legendary leaders, both on the trail and in the bars of Kathmandu and elsewhere. Together we were in a small, closely-knit world of enthusiasts who had both a passion for the mountains and an enthusiasm to share the adventure with others. Different companies might be competing for clients, but in the mountains we were all friends.

Such was the success of Karakoram Experience that in 1996 they changed the company name to KE Adventure Travel to reflect the global range of trekking, climbing and mountain biking trips that they by then offered.

Following the shock of the collapse of OTT/Alpine Mountaineering I wasn't quite sure what to do next. Of one thing I was certain, I needed a break from organising and leading trips to 8000m peaks. I was torn between returning to a more conventional life or seeking to reconnect with the joy that trekking, exploring and climbing had brought me before, both doing my own trips and leading others in slightly less hostile and dangerous places. Really I wanted both. Rather than decide one way or the other I tried both routes, rather anticipating that destiny would determine which way I would go. I applied for the job working in the Chief Executive's Department of Nottingham City Council and to lead some climbing and trekking trips for KE Adventure Travel. It wasn't a very good strategy: I got offered work by both. Still in the throes of indecision, I accepted both. For KE I managed to squeeze in and co-lead one really enjoyable trip to Mera Peak, the Amphu Labsta and Island Peak in Nepal. Afterwards I wrote in my diary that it was:

"My first and maybe my last trip for KE."

I then began full-time permanent employment with Nottingham City Council on 10th December 2001. I often say to people who join a trek or climb that what they may anticipate as a trip of a lifetime is actually addictive and for most people they do return or at least dream of doing so. I've been hooked for 35 years. A large percentage of KE clients are also repeat clients.

I knew that I would miss the life and the adventure but I also knew that I would enjoy and value more conventional home, family and working life. It was an especially interesting time to be working for the local authority as it struggled under the leadership of a new Chief Executive to improve the quality of service and value for money that it gave to the people of the City.

Unfortunately, the forces for change and the forces of resistance met and the politicians fell out with the Chief Executive - or the other way round. It matters little now. The result was that after I had been in the organisation less than a year he was sacked. My own job immediately lacked at the very least focus and direction (or it may even have been destined not to exist) after the arrival of a replacement.

Shortly after that, Janet was invited to apply for a job in a part-British Government-funded project in Beijing. She got the job. So about fourteen months after deciding that conventional employment was the right course, on 1st February 2003 we moved to China. We let our Victorian suburban house in Sheffield and moved to a new apartment on the 29th Floor of Tower A Global Trade Mansions in central Beijing. We lived there until December 2004.

My visa, which was changed at the last minute, allowed me to work in China but was not a Diplomatic one that would allow me to work for the British Embassy or similar English-speaking organisations, so in effect as I didn't even speak a word of Mandarin at the time, I would have to work outside the country. It was a different sort of adventure.

Within days of our arrival Andy Broom emailed me to explain that a lot of former clients and expedition leaders from the OTT/Alpine Mountaineering days would like me to organise their Everest, Lhotse and Nuptse expeditions for spring 2002. In exchange I would definitely (this time) be put on a permit to climb something. Somehow in the excitement I seemed to forget the promise that I had made to myself about not organising more expeditions and accepted. The permit started off as being for Everest, although I wouldn't be a member of any group. In the end I was alone on a permit to climb Everest's large neighbour Lhotse (8516m). It was far from ideal.

The mountain was especially busy in 2003, it being the 50th anniversary of the first ascent, and there were 800+ people due to occupy Base Camp. They were from 22 expeditions plus the inevitable rabble of TV and film crews etc.

American Mountain Guide Scott Woolums (from Hood River in Oregon), whom I had known since Cho Oyu days, had a team for both Everest and Lhotse. Pat Falvey (who had summited Cho Oyu on my first trip there in 1998) had an Irish Everest Team. The Patagonia Brothers (twins Willie and Damian Benegas) had ambitions for a new and difficult route on

Nuptse, and Damian's then girlfriend Edurne Pasabanm, who went on to become one of the first women to climb all 8000m peaks, was going for Lhotse with a small team from her home in the Basque country. It was a stressful and thankless job to ensure that everything that was needed to feed and support all four expeditions arrived in time, but it did. Just.

When everything was finally in order I began my own solo ascent. Of course it was not really solo as much of the ordinary route up the mountain was relatively crowded with other groups of climbers, and the route was well rigged with ropes and ladders, but nonetheless I was an independent team of one.

I climbed the Khumbu Icefall several times to acclimatise and spent nights in Camp 1 (6000m) at the top of it. I then moved on across the wide and crevassed glacier of the Western Cwm. Camp 2 sits at the head of the valley at the base of Everest's South-West Face, the route of Chris Bonington's 1975 expedition. For me though, much more poignant was the easy and safe looking ground around the tents at Camp 2 which had hidden the crevasse that killed Babu Chhiri in 2001.

Things start to get steep above Camp 2 as the route progresses up the Geneva Spur and the Lhotse Face. All the climbing is on fixed ropes but deaths have occurred here when climbers have become over-confident and fallen hundreds of metres. I spent a night at Camp 3 at about 7100m with the tent perched on a precarious ledge. For me climbing like this required me to concentrate on my every action. I remember it was thrilling rather than scary and feeling quite pleased with myself as I lay huddled in my sleeping bag with the wind blowing hard outside, feeling that I had things under control.

In the morning the weather wasn't looking good so I descended to Base Camp and on downwards to the village of

Pheriche to rest at a lower altitude. After a couple of nights of rest at lower altitude, during which time I also bumped into my friend Mick Bromley leading a KE group in the area, I headed back up to the mountain with the aim of climbing it.

I spent another night at Base Camp and then went back up again through the tottering ice cliffs of the Khumbu Icefall (which I climbed a total of six times during the expedition, during which time several ladders collapsed and the safest route had to be remade). By then I was feeling fitter and more acclimatised and so bypassed Camp 1 and pushed on directly to Camp 2. When I got there it was great to see the friendly faces of Phanden and the other sherpas.

At the time Phanden was effortlessly hacking a ledge out of the rock and ice to make another tent platform. I tried to help, but very soon realised yet again that the sherpas are in a different league of fitness at altitude. I collapsed onto the snow gasping for breath.

Nonetheless, I was feeling relatively strong and optimistic about the climb ahead. Beyond my previous high point at Camp 3 the route crosses the Yellow Band. I t is a layer of limestone that runs across the mountain and is a famous marker on the way to the South Col and the normal route on Everest. My route would not take me all the way to the South Col but turn sharply before it and lead up a series of steep rocky gullies towards the summit of Lhotse.

In my early years in the Himalaya and Karakoram Janet and I exchanged lengthy letters and we both still have them as souvenirs of those times. By 2002 it was however possible to just call home on the satellite telephone. It sounds like a good and convenient idea but it is a mixed blessing. I am nearly always overcome with emotion and am on the brink of tears, irrespective of whether I'm just back from a summit or am still really struggling upwards.

I called Janet from Camp 2. It was of course fantastic to talk to her, but at one level must just have added to her anxiety knowing that I was just about to head off up the Lhotse Face alone. It also caused a change in me. It could be either be described as it breaking my concentration and therefore my ability to continue with what I was doing, or perhaps non-mountaineering observers might have said it made me see sense. It made me question what I was doing up there. Of course, as soon as those sorts of questions appear in your consciousness, it's all over.

I did go back up to Camp 3 and spent the night sharing a tent with two of Scott Woolums' team. In the morning they set off using bottled oxygen. I tried but found it more difficult with it than without it. When I reached the Yellow Band I realised that I had run out of oomph. Not physical oomph, but psychological oomph. It was time to go home.

Some members of Scott's and Pat's teams reached the summit, but the big news stories were that Edurne moved one step closer to climbing all the 8000m peaks and Willie and Damian climbed a magnificent and technical new ice route on Nuptse (7861m) that they called The Crystal Snake.

Soon after I returned to Beijing, Fiona Marshall (the Operations person at KE) emailed me to ask whether I would be interested in leading a trip to Lhakpa Ri in Tibet. At 7045m on the other side of the East Rongbuk Glacier from Everest, and a key feature in Mallory's early explorations of the mountain, how could I not be?

At the time it was also the highest summit offered on a KE trip. Pasang Sherpa (one of the top sherpas working with KE) and I got three clients on two ropes to the summit and back in good order. Things felt right again and I wrapped up the year with KE with a couple of treks in the Khumbu Region of Nepal.

I slowly began not to feel like I was the new boy in the KE team and opportunities to lead trips kept on coming. In the spring of 2004 I led another trip to Mera Peak (6461m), my seventh, and then a trek to the Goecha La near Kangchenjunga in Sikkim, India.

In the summer I was asked to lead three trips back-to-back in Mongolia. I had never been to Mongolia, but soon learned that there were remote and isolated alpine size heavily glaciated mountains along the west and north-west frontiers of the country where it butted on to Russia and China. Two of the trips involved climbing several peaks in the Altai Tavan Bogd in the west and one was a trek in the north.

For the first climbing trip I teamed up with my friend Ade Summers, a Welsh Australian and Mongolia enthusiast. Unfortunately, the weather was very poor and despite spending a day hauling all our camping gear and equipment up the Potanin Glacier, the wind was too strong for us to pitch the tents on the ice and make a high camp, so we had no choice but to descend. We were all a bit disappointed.

On the evening before we were due to leave Base Camp however the weather looked slightly better, so I suggested to the group that we could still attempt the main peak Mount Khuiten (4374m). In the end I had two volunteers. We would have to leave after dinner, trek roped-up back up the Potanin Glacier to our high point of the previous day, climb through the night and perhaps reach the summit just before dawn. The climbing would be on snow and ice and include some steep ground and pitched climbing, using ice screws as protection. We would aim to retrace our steps and get back to Base Camp in time for breakfast. After breakfast a local herder would bring some

Mongolian ponies for the whole group to ride back to the road-head. The gear would be carried by camels. We would reach the road head in time for dinner in the evening. The following day we would drive off-road for twelve hours to the dusty township of Bayan Olgii from where we would return by plane to the capital Ulaan Bataar the next day. And that is pretty much what happened, with me and Ade taking clients Gordon from Scotland and Marc from Hawaii on a very extended long day out that began on the 7th and ended on the 9th July! Sometimes it is just right to go for it.

On the second climbing trip in the same place that summer, a similar thing happened again except it involved a shorter day, a slightly lower and easier peak called Narindal and a team including Janet and our friends Janet Moore (with whom I had climbed in Pakistan in the 1980s), Angela Tod and Neil and Lorraine Roden.

Not every KE trip goes exactly according to the advertised itinerary. The company name is after all suffixed by the term "adventure travel". Since then I have returned to Mongolia many times, and I too am a Mongolia enthusiast.

In the autumn I took another group to the summit of Lhakpa Ri in Tibet and led a trek in the Khumbu. To round things off, towards the end of the season my long-time friends Phanden Sherpa, Ade Summers and I fancied doing a trip just for ourselves. Ade is usually as tough as old boots (in a good way!) but unfortunately as he had only just arrived in Nepal he was a bit struck down by the altitude, so Phanden and I climbed to just below the summit of Parchemo (6187m) together. It was the peak in the Khumbu on which Joe and Mal Duff had their accident after climbing a new route in the spring of 1991.

During the autumn back in Kathmandu, something else was happening, but I didn't know anything about it until it was sprung on me. At the heart of many of the most adventurous trips run by KE there has always been a core of nearly full-time leaders. They have a fantastic depth of knowledge and enthusiasm for the places they travel, trek and climb. When I first came across KE back in the 1980s Steve Razetti and Pete Royal were two such stalwarts. They are still key personalities in the organisation. Later others took on the role including a young chap called Ian Wade.

To describe Ian was quite easy. He had a ZZ Top-type long beard, always wore a baseball cap, had loads of tattoos and a big, warm, open smile. He was and is one of the most hilarious story tellers I've ever met. He broached the idea that we should organise an Everest Expedition for KE Leaders and long-time Sherpa friends for 2005. I thought it was a good one. Then, as an afterthought, he added that I would be the leader. This time he wasn't joking and, once again forgetting my pledge, I agreed.

As well as snatching success from the jaws of defeat on KE trips, things can also sometimes go wrong. Even the relatively frequently climbed smaller peaks in the Everest Area can become scenes of high drama. One example was on a trip with a big itinerary that included walking up the view point of Gokyo Ri, crossing the glaciated pass of the Cho La, climbing Lobuche Peak (6119m), walking up the view point near Everest Base Camp called Kala Pattar, crossing the pass of the Kongma La climbing Pokalde Peak (5806m) and then finishing off with climbing Island Peak (more correctly called Imja Tse) (6189m).

Towards the end of the trip, having been at altitude for a couple of weeks and on our last objective, we left our high camp in the dark in the early hours of the morning to climb Island Peak. The route is in four sections: a steep walk to some rocky scrambling that leads to the edge of a glacier, from where crampons and axes are used and the teams move together roped up, carefully avoiding the crevasses. The glacier leads to a steep icy headwall. Usually a series of fixed ropes are attached to aid and safeguard the ascent and descent. From the top of the headwall a narrow ridge leads to a small summit with spectacular views in all directions, but most especially of the north side of Ama Dablam.

We had reached about halfway up the final head wall when one of the group members said that he felt faint and unwell. I had descended with him a few days earlier from near the summit of Lobuche, but he had subsequently crossed several passes and climbed Pokalde Peak. I instructed the Sirdar or lead Sherpa Lhakpa and the assistant leader to continue with the other members of the group to the summit. Pemba, another of the Sherpas and I helped the client down the fixed ropes. By the time we reached the easier angle of the glacier it was obvious that he was suffering from a high altitude cerebral oedema. By the time we got to the edge of the glacier and I removed his crampons he could hardly stand unaided.

Carefully, but with a sense of urgency, we helped him down the steep rocky sections, trying to keep talking to him to check the state of his deterioration. He was moving as if he was drunk and slurring his speech. Safety was still a long way away. By the time we reached High Camp he could not even sit upright. I administered the appropriate medications. Our office in Kathmandu was called on the satellite telephone to arrange for an urgent helicopter evacuation. The site of the High Camp is too steep for a helicopter to land so Pemba and I started to carry him in turn on our backs down the steep, loose moraine to the Base Camp. He probably weighed more than me and about 30% more than Pemba.

We called our office again to check progress, but were told that the weather was too bad for a helicopter to land and not to expect one until the next day. We had to continue to carry him down to the nearest settlement at Chhukhung, several miles away and over some difficult rocky terrain. Whenever we stopped for a rest he just slumped on the ground. I knew we would be OK but only if we could get him down fast enough. The pressure was on. Then, thankfully, the rest of our Sherpa and cook team arrived. Lakpa had taken the group to the summit, escorted them back to the High Camp and, leaving them with the rest of the crew, had rushed down and caught us up, bringing a bit more muscle power. They chopped up one of the traditional baskets that Nepali people use to carry loads by a single strap around their forehead, tied the client in it and we all set off at a jog. I could only just keep up. We were still at about 5000m.

In addition to the altitude medicines and the satellite telephone, I also had a Gamow Pressure bag into which a sufferer can be placed and which, by pumping the air pressure, can be raised to simulate a descent of many hundreds of metres. We eventually reached the settlement of Chhukhung and after administering rehydration and further medication, I sat all night next to him as he slept. If he had deteriorated further we would have had no choice but to carry him further down to a lower altitude during the night or use the Gamow Bag. In the morning the helicopter did arrive and he was soon whisked to hospital in Kathmandu.

When we met up again, he had been discharged and was feeling fine. He had no recollection of the events on the mountain and was in denial about the extent of his illness. There is no doubt that without his evacuation and the drugs he would have died hanging from the rope on the headwall of Island Peak within the hour. This was not a unique experience. Most people, but not everyone, given enough time and attention to some basic rules can acclimatise to 6000m or so. It seems to me that the people who are at greatest risk are often young, fit men who, full of competitiveness and testosterone, deny the symptoms and push on. Some very experienced mountaineers who are going to altitude for the first time also suffer as somehow they expect that their experience will make them immune too. Others who worry too much about getting ill can, it seems to me, bring it on. It can be a difficult balance to strike.

Since joining KE over a decade ago I have led fifty trips for them, mainly in the Himalaya and Karakoram, but also in other parts of Asia and North and East Africa. I have learned a lot and am still in the process of doing so. All the trips have been an absolute delight and it is an on-going pleasure and obviously a great privilege to be able to help others to have an adventure of a lifetime.

Do I have an ambition? Well at the end of 2004 I certainly did. I wanted to organise, lead and hopefully reach the summit of Everest with my UK and Nepalese KE friends in the spring of the following year.

Chapter 11

Out as Friends, Back as Friends

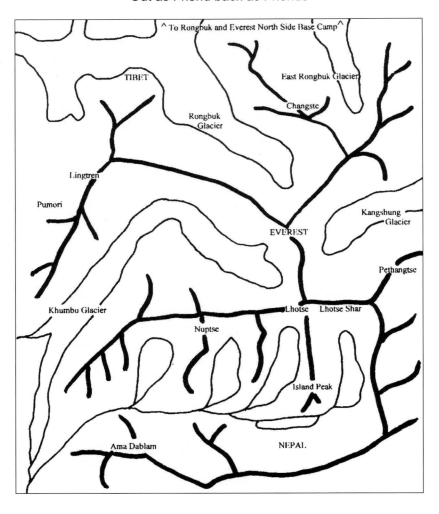

Map of Everest

Everest has always been different. Even back in 1953 the great mountaineer and explorer Eric Shipton thought so. He had been partially responsible for persuading the powers that be at the time that the most likely route to the summit was not as all pre-war expeditions had tried, from the North in Tibet, but via the Khumbu Glacier, the so called Western Cwm and the South Col in Nepal.

Despite Shipton being the world authority on the mountain (and the fact that the Swiss had more or less climbed it the previous year anyway) he was removed from being the leader and was replaced by a military man, Colonel John Hunt. So understandably he may have been a little bitter about the whole saga, and once Everest had been climbed he was credited with saying something like:

"Well at least we can get back to real climbing now."

He had a point then. An Everest Expedition had become a national or nationalist campaign or even a war with no enemy and, like the attempts to reach the South Pole, a symbol of the enduring power of the British Empire (even though in reality by 1953 the Empire was fading fast). Some people in Britain even thought that climbing Everest was a part of the Queen's Coronation ceremony. It had temporarily lost the freedom, excitement, adventure and delight that mountaineering offers elsewhere.

In a slightly different way the inference made in Shipton's remark about how we see Everest and what we do on it is also true these days. The vast majority of expeditions to Everest are now run by commercial organisations with paying clients, and some pay big bucks too. I know - I have organised several. A few others are, if not national teams, I would say niche teams such as "The first Iranian Women's Expedition" (which although planned didn't happen due to the invasion of Iraq), "First Everest Expedition on which a blind man will reach the summit" (he was Erik Weihenmayer), or the first pogo stick ascent of Everest, which I just made up to show where things might go. It makes for a strange population and a mix of highly charged egos at Base Camps.

We on the other hand were going to do it the old-fashioned way, the way most mountaineering with the exception of to Everest is done. We were going out as a group of mates. The three big differences would be that whatever happened we would almost certainly have a good time, that because we were friends we would also be very keen to look after and out for each other, and it would be far, far cheaper, or at least less expensive. Why doesn't everyone do it that way?

I was informed that a democratic decision had been made (in which I didn't have a vote) that I was to be the Leader. We would be a team of twelve with eight of us being KE Leaders and four being KE Sherpas. In addition we would have a cook and cook team and a doctor, but more on that in a moment.

We would climb the mountain from the north, the Tibet

side. We had two reasons for this. At the time it was cheaper and less crowded and, unlike on the south side, there is not a dangerous section of glacier low down like the Khumbu Icefall that has to be crossed many times. On the other hand the hardest climbing is, as Mallory and Irvine and more recently Conrad Ankar and Leo Houlding found out, quite near the top.

The other big difference is that, like other very high mountains, you cannot just start from the bottom and keep climbing until you reach the top. In effect you have to build yourself and a supply chain up the mountain, making camps, shuttling supplies up and acclimatising until you can make your attempt. It is a style that rock climbers might call Red Pointing, as opposed to Flashing it.

On our trip Tim Calder was to be the Assistant Leader. He would be a handy chap to have about. He was an ex-Ghurkha who spoke fluent Nepali, was very strong in the mountains and, even better, lived in Kathmandu. After a couple of months however Tim decided that he would rather be working and paid on a commercial expedition than having to pay to join one, so he joined Henry Todd as the Co-leader of his trip on the Nepal side.

Several months of preparation in the UK and Nepal arranging permission, radios, tents, oxygen and so on followed. Then a team comprising Mick Bromley, Pasang, Phanden, Jangbu and Karma Sherpas and I then spent a week in Kathmandu prior to the arrival of the others, buying provisions and dealing with the administration. Mick also took on the unenviable role of dealing with the budget. As well as leading KE trips and doing his own climbing, he was from time to time a maths teacher, so was, we concluded, likely to be more numerate than the rest of us. In the end our costs were about 25% of those of a commercial expedition and $90 out from his original estimate. Considering that we were on an expedition of seventy days with twelve climbers, a cook, kitchen crew and a doctor and we had to take everything we needed by road into Tibet and then by yak up to the mountain and then climb it, it was an amazing achievement. Mick now lives in Canada running a company called Wilderness Trekking. We miss him personally and the UK more than ever needs a decent Chancellor of the Exchequer if he ever comes back!

One of my favourite tasks prior to any expedition leaving Kathmandu is meeting with Elizabeth Hawley. Liz, an American who originally worked as a journalist for Fortune Magazine, has lived in Kathmandu for more than four decades and has developed the definitive data base, although it wasn't called that then, of mountaineering in the Himalaya. She has never been a mountaineer but her knowledge is such that through her questioning she always gets to the truth. Allegedly some of the greatest mountaineers in the world have feared her "sharp tongue and relentless questioning" and never get beyond referring to her humbly and respectfully as "Miss Hawley". I have always found her helpful, charming and delightful. I am also always amazed that within thirty minutes of arriving at my hotel from the airport at the beginning of a trip she calls me to make an appointment to meet. How does she know I'm there?

Even now, in her 80s, she is still carrying on gathering and reporting on events and still living in Kathmandu. So we met and I told her all about our plans for what had become labelled, due to a bit of support from my friend Ewan Bruce at Karrimor in the form of Karrimats, rucksacks and duffle bags, the Karrimor Everest Expedition 2005.

On 1st April a partially complete team, now also including mountaineer, paraglider and photographer extraordinaire Stuart Holmes and our cook Robbie Dyke, left Kathmandu (altitude 1400m) by road travelling in two trucks and three Land Cruisers. All the vehicles were clearly labelled "Tourists Only" to avoid being attacked by the local Maoists for breaking their anti-government transport strikes. We spent the first night near the border with Tibet amongst terraced fields and rich subtropical vegetation. In the evening Ian Wade and ex-soldier and outdoor instructor Ross Ash-Cregan also caught up, as planned.

The next day we had to pass through the lengthy formalities at the China/Tibet border at the village of Zangmu. One of the officials, apparently realising that my passport was issued in Beijing, China, where I had lived at the time, engaged me in conversation. He was a long way from home. I tried a bit of my Mandarin, he responded in fluent English. He then collected up the passports of everyone in the queue and disappeared into his office. To pass the time I chatted to the guy in front of me. He was unusual in this part of the world as he was black and said he came from Ghana. There are not many people from Ghana who have visited Tibet, I mused. Moments later my other conversational partner, the Chinese Official came out of his office and walked straight over to me. He gave me my passport back.

"What do you think of this?", he asked, showing me the picture page of the Ghanaian chap's passport? "Nothing" I replied. Then he held the passport up so the blazing sunlight light shone across the page. "I think he has a problem," said the official. I thought we were about to experience some Chinese racism. "I will show you here because if I do it in the office everyone will say I tricked him," he continued. Carefully over several minutes he picked away at the laminate on the photo page and slowly peeled the plastic away. When the plastic peeled off it was plain to see that there was another picture underneath the portrait of the man who still stood next to me. It was of a white man.

The official then flicked through the other pages; the man did not have an exit visa stamp to leave Nepal either. It did seem strange. After a few words both of them turned silently and walked into his office. My head was swimming with a mix of emotions, my own stereotyping had drawn me first in one direction and then another. A rare friendly Chinese official, what looked as if it was going to be a simple vulgar act of racism and then apparently a stolen identity and a pointless bit of fraud? Was what I had just seen what really happened or had I been a part of some elaborate hoax? I'll never know. I never saw either of them again.

Eventually, having cleared the officials and the town, we made our way along the crumbling narrow road high above the Sun Kosi river gorge. Towards the end it went through a long, seven metre-high snowdrift through which a truck-sized slot had recently been bulldozed. The next day we crossed passes at over 5000m on the then unmade up road. It's a tough journey and certainly one with plenty of contrast.

Finally, after six days of driving and acclimatisation, we arrived at Base Camp. The mountain looks magnificent from the Base Camp. It is, to be frank, much more impressive than from the Nepal side.

Our cook Robbie Dyke, a friend of Mick's, then began work. Usually we would have a Nepali cook but Robbie was very keen and an amiable chap. He was from Canada and his two passions in life were swimming and cooking. Later in the summer of 2005 he was to be the first person to swim round Vancouver Island. And he thought that mountaineering was mad!

His plan was to cook for us at Base Camp and at Advanced Base Camp (ABC) at 6400m and then to write the definitive Everest Cook Book. Unfortunately on his first foray up on the two day trek to ABC he became ill. The others were keen to push on to ABC. I didn't like the idea of Robbie going back alone so I descended with him and subsequently had to look after him for several days at Base Camp. After that he remained there for the duration of the trip, still a tough enough and lonely place to be in the cold and constant wind.

Our doctor was also a Canadian citizen. He was a Professor of Surgery and much else in Toronto. More importantly though, Dr John Semple, or Dr John as he became known (in honour of the American Blues/Jazz musician who performed under the same name), was a keen mountaineer and trekker and personally interested in altitude medicine research. That plus the fact that he was a really nice guy was enough for us. All the rest of us were used to dealing with mountain medicine issues ourselves on KE trips so it was a relief to be able to concentrate more on the mountain. Dr John also provided a weather forecast service by text on our satellite phone from Canada. We charged the satellite phone and our radios using a solar panel that trickle charged a car battery brought by truck and yak from Kathmandu.

It was not until 24th April that the final members of our team arrived at Base Camp. Matt Sharman worked in the KE office as well as leading trips. He couldn't be spared from the office for the duration of the trip, apparently. His long time friend, artist and KE leader Dan Short had chosen to travel out with him too. With them was Tim Mosedale, a climbing instructor from Keswick who had joined at the last minute to take the slot left by Tim Calder. In the meantime the rest of us had already got most of the gear and supplies sorted and carried by yak up to ABC and, having rested, had also climbed up to the North Col. Pasang, Phanden, Karma and Jangbu were far ahead and already supplying the location that would become Camp 2. I first reached Camp 1 on the North Col on 20th April and then, after a few nights at ABC, on the 23rd I walked the six hours back down to Base Camp at 5300m.

On the 27th I went back up, spending one night at our halfway camp before reaching ABC again on 28th. I was amazed as I struggled into camp to meet Jangbu and Karma arriving back from the site of Camp 3 at about 8300m. They had dumped some supplies. For Karma it was his first big mountain expedition and he seemed to have a natural talent for it.

On the 1st May I was back again and set off up towards the North Col once more with the aim of assisting Dr John to reach it. After nearly four hours we had only just reached the bottom of the fixed ropes, normally less than an hour from ABC where the steeper ground begins. We returned to ABC. On the 3rd May I climbed back up to the North Col. I wrote in my diary:

"8 am climb to Camp 1 on the North Col. Not going very well. Arrived just behind Ross who left camp 15 minutes after me (and he's older than me). A bit disappointed and frustrated at my own performance. But it is only my second time up."

The next day I attempted to carry some supplies towards Camp 2 on the North Ridge, or more accurately *a* supply - just one bottle of Russian-made oxygen. Phanden, Pasang, Karma, Jangbu and Ian took two and Mick picked up an extra one from Stuart when he turned back. Ross and I dumped ours in the snow at a point a bit below the site of the Camp. It was hard work but the views were just as breathtaking. To our right we could look down to the Nepal side of the mountains. The popular Everest trekking route was laid out clearly below us like a map and to its right and below where we stood was Pumo Ri, the mountain I visited in 1991 and 1995. Directly dropping away below my feet was the Main Rongbuk Glacier and the evocatively named snowfield called the White Limbo that smears itself between the two great couloirs that split Everest's North face, the Great and the Hornbein.

It felt like a fairly good start and over the next two days we all returned again to the relatively lower altitudes of Base Camp to rest. Whilst resting at Base Camp I took a walk to visit the nearby cluster of memorial stones. There were lots of them in the area , including one to Mallory and Irvine. Further away there were many others including to Pete Boardman and Joe Tasker, who disappeared trying to make the first ascent of the North-East Ridge in 1982. Further on there was another, newer sign. It commemorated Marco Siffredi, the strong and friendly young French snowboarder who had given me some encouraging words as he bounded past me on the way to the summit of Cho Oyu, only to snowboard back down it in great style. He died trying to descend a couloir on his snowboard, the one I had seen only a few days earlier, the Hornbein Couloir. I just wrote in my diary:

"So many people gone."

I also visited my friend and, although he didn't and still doesn't know this, my high altitude expeditioning mentor Russell Brice. We discussed how our small team might be able to contribute to the massive task and cost of fixing ropes on the mountain that he co-ordinates on behalf of other expeditions on the mountain. He is widely known to be the most professional and successful operator in the world of commercial high altitude expeditions. In addition, amongst many other achievements, with Harry Taylor he was also the first to climb the pinnacles on the North-East Ridge of Everest, past the place where Pete Boardman and Joe Tasker disappeared.

Later we were also visited at our camp by Ian Parnell. He was a member of the new generation of young British Alpinists who were once again making their mark on the world climbing scene. He had been engaged as the photographer for the charity fundraiser and former polar explorer Ranulph Fiennes. Ian later summited Everest but Ranulph Fiennes did

211

not, at least not that year. In 2010, having become a father, Ian would take over a new role and become the Assistant Editor on Climb magazine and become another of my many employers.

The weather then broke. The forecast wasn't very encouraging either. However by the evening of the 16th May we were all back at ABC to be prepared for a window of good weather should it occur. The word was that some of the Sherpas working for a Norwegian group had, despite counsel from Russell Brice that they should wait for the weather to improve, been instructed to climb above the current high point and continue fixing ropes. They reached the second step but did get some frost bite damage. An Irish couple who had planned to marry on the summit didn't make it either. One of them suffered retinal blood clots so they had to give up and descend, hopefully only temporarily blind and still unmarried.

A KE group on a Tibet Tour visited Base Camp and very kindly left us a barrel of goodies. Their departure was an escape route for Robbie too and he decided that enough was enough and elected to return to Kathmandu with them. Amongst other things I guess he had to prepare for swimming around Vancouver Island.

On the 18th I returned again to the North Col and back in deteriorating weather, this time with Mick, Matt and Dan and also, because he really wanted to have a go, one of the boys from the kitchen, Chandra. I seemed to be going well having had a rest lower down at Base Camp. I reached the col in 3 hours 40 minutes from ABC.

A Leaders' meeting was held in Russell's Camp. There was a lot of bad feeling towards him from some groups. They were demanding that he send his sherpas up to fix the ropes to the summit. He was clear that he wasn't going to put them at such risk while the weather was bad. Some of them, including the Indian Air force team, seemed to be taking a paying customer point of view, i.e. we contributed some money or ropes so you must do what we want. Other groups, who had not even made a contribution in terms of Sherpa power, money or ropes, moaned at him as well. It was a great demonstration of Russell's knowledge and judgement and his primary concern for the safety of his and everybody else's Sherpas and clients that he held his ground. The whole thing seemed to me to be a very tough way for Russell to earn a living and others' behaviour a long way from the ethos of mountaineering at its best. Personally I think that on this and every other occasion over the years that we have been on a mountain together, Russell has contributed more to everyone's safety than could possibly be expected. He is one of the few professionals in the business.

Dr John's weather forecast said that we would have a clear patch of weather until the 24th. It could be our only chance to go for it? Sobering us still further, two Koreans were later carried down past our Camp. I called Janet on the satellite phone to tell her I was off up, a selfish act on my part that must have just heightened her anxiety.

On the evening of the 19th we are all assembled at the North Col ready to start for the summit via Camps 2 and 3 the next day. However on our radio call to Dr John we found the good weather forecast was cancelled and, as if to prove it, it snowed. The next morning, deflated, we went down.

On the morning of 21st at ABC, after a long period of persuasion, Ross headed down and for home. He had been feeling pain in his calf for days and had all the symptoms of a deep vein thrombosis brought on by altitude. He needed to descend and get medical assistance at a lower altitude, and the sooner the better.

The weather was clear but windy and we spotted some figures on the area of the summit pyramid. It was rumoured that this time it was the sherpas from the Indian Air Force expedition. The officers at ABC had also decided that Russell's plan of waiting for the weather to clear was not correct. I suppose that the outcome of such expeditions has an effect on the CVs of both the officers and men involved on these things. What a horrible pressure to feel that you are put under.

On the 22nd the sky was again clear but it was cold and windy. We heard reports that twenty-five Chinese climbers had reached the summit and that one Russian had died, but who knows? Base Camp was as full of rumours as it was of people. We saw little of the Chinese group and the only lasting reminder was the mountain of rubbish at ABC that they left at their Camp site at the end of the expedition. Everyone else took theirs down for disposal when they left.

In the late afternoon a Tibetan yak herder arrived. His job was to take down the large blue plastic barrels that every group used as their toilet. He was required to empty them lower down at an altitude in which the contents would compost down. He was then at liberty to use or sell the barrels. Unfortunately we thought for him, but actually for us, our barrel wasn't full. The next morning, before first light, we discovered that during the night he had stolen not only our barrel and its contents but those of several other expeditions as well!

Several of our team were beginning to get worn down by being at altitude for so long. Bronchial and stomach infections or upsets do not respond as well to medications and, even if symptomless, everyone, including the ever strong foursome of Pasang, Phanden, Jangbu and Karma, was getting tired. The rumour was that many groups attempting the mountain from the Nepal side would be aiming to reach the summit on the 30th or 31st. The text weather forecast confirmed that the weather was indeed going to be fine.

On the 27th we all set off once more back up to the now familiar North Col. I wrote in my diary that, "I was exhausted just setting off from ABC and took 4 hours to reach the North Col. I shared a tent with Tim who was going strong and full of beans having shaken off a chest infection."

We all set off again the next morning, carrying our personal gear up to spend the night at Camp 2, summit bound. One terrifying few moments was when a snowboarder slid down the crest of the ridge past me. I don't know where he had come from, the summit or a higher camp. I didn't dare to look at him, let alone speak in case I distracted him and the balancing seesaw action of his snowboard along the snow edge overbalanced and plunged him the many hundreds of metres down the drop on either side. Later again in my diary I wrote:

"A very tough day for me up the snow of the North Ridge and around the rocks to Camp 2. Very windy with wild clouds coming up from the south."

Could this be the arrival of the monsoon, I wondered? Stuart, usually stronger than me, struggled up to camp, stopping regularly due to an attack of diarrhoea, a problem that is not easy to deal with on a steep snow slope, wearing a down suit at 7500m.

Mick and Matt came in last. As ever Mick was going strong but kept alongside his friend Matt who was, like most of us struggling. Stuart and I shared a tent and decided that to help us to rest we would sleep using a slow flow of bottled oxygen.

I had a bad night, not because I couldn't sleep but because we had very successfully rehydrated ourselves with several drinks and food. To deal with the problem of peeing it is normal to have a pee bottle to use inside your tent and sleeping bag. It is a skilled and high risk operation. The rule is to empty your pee bottle outside the tent after you have used it. I didn't think that I was that well rehydrated so didn't apply it. In my altitude-addled state I used it again. It overflowed into my sleeping bag and over my down suit. I had no choice but to sleep in it. It was probably more than 45 years since I had last wet my bed! The next morning it turned out not to be as bad as I had thought. As soon as I turned my sleeping bag inside out, the wetness froze and the ice could just be shaken off.

The weather was still wild and windy. All of us agreed to wait and see if it improved and not to move off until 11am. I was feeling increasingly exhausted and had a sore throat. I talked to Phanden before he left with the other Sherpas. He said, "Tom Dhai, too much hard work, too many days at ABC and now too old!" It was a tough message to hear and one which only a good friend can tell you, but at the time I had to agree. I was 50 and had never felt so tired. Nonetheless, don't ask me why, I prepared to head on up slowly to Camp 3. Dan had already decided to go down and had left earlier in the morning. Tim and Ian left next, but heading upwards and looking strong. Ian said he had a sore throat. Stuart followed, now apparently recovered, and was followed by Mick and Matt who were just aiming to tick 8000m. Mick was still not using bottled oxygen. I started off with it but it is so unwieldy and unpleasant I soon gave up too. The face mask prevents you from seeing your feet and it seemed easier to just gasp and pant than to only breathe the oxygen from the bottle in my pack. Enough oxygen must have reached my brain for me to realise that, although I felt that I could possibly reach Camp 3 at 8300m, I would not be going any further. It was pointless. It was time to go down.

I turned, clipped a sling to the fixed lines and began to descend. Almost immediately I felt as if I had run out of power, or been somehow deflated. Adrenaline can keep you going upwards but the high point is only halfway. After just a few minutes I had to sit down and rest.

It took me some time to reach the tents on the now familiar North Col. From there I abseiled and slid down the ropes towards ABC. The middle section of the route is the steepest. In my bleary state I dropped my figure of eight abseiling device. Fortunately I was not so out of it to unclip from the rope and clamber down to get it from the snow ledge a couple of metres below me. Instead I had to summon all my powers of concentration to abseil down the ropes using an Italian Hitch. I was very relieved to reach the bottom. What had been an easy stroll across the glacier and down the moraine path back to ABC earlier in the trip was another struggle. Much to my delight Dr John, Dan and Chandra were on their way up the moraine to meet me. They had some warm drink. I tried to speak but, due to my sore throat, exhaustion and gasping in the cold air for so long, I had no voice and could only croak my appreciation.

The next morning the first radio call was from Phanden at 6am. He was on the summit of Everest with Jangbu and Karma. It was his first time from the north, although he had reached it from the Nepal side several times. I was really pleased for him and a big part of me wished I had been strong enough on the day to be up there with him. I couldn't really reply though as I still was voiceless so I had to whisper my responses to Dr John to speak for me. Shortly after that I received another call, this time from Tim and Stuart. They were on the summit and doing well. I asked about how the ever-strong Ian was doing. They replied that he was going slowly but surely, climbing with Pasang. They all passed Ian and Pasang, still moving upwards as they descended.

The next radio call was from Ian. He reached the summit several hours after the others and he reminded me it was his 31st birthday. His voice sounded unusually frail but he had made it.

Some time later I heard his voice again on the radio. They were on their way down and had reached the top of the Second Step. It is the most technical part of the route down which most people abseiled. Ian told me that he had gone partially blind. Pasang was still with him and that they would come down carefully together. His voice was trembling.

Ian had got retinal bleeding caused by the altitude. Sometimes it is permanent and complete and sometimes with time and treatment it can be cured. Up there above 8400m it didn't matter either way: his life was on the line. We called the others who were either on their way to or had just arrived at Camp 3. We had made good preparations, everyone had an emergency altitude kit and Camp 3 had plenty of oxygen, fuel and help for anyone if they needed it. The next call was not from Ian, but from Pasang. Ian had collapsed at the bottom of the ropes at the base of the Second Step.

Stuart later described events on our blog:

"Our hearts stopped, our minds raced. What could we do from here? To climb back up would take hours. Dr John was talking to Pasang on the radio explaining that he had to draw 2cc of dexamethazone (let's hope it's not frozen) and inject it into Ian's leg. In the end Ian came round enough to do it himself.

Within 5 minutes the drug had taken effect and Ian was able to stand and eventually make progress down. At Camp 3 Phanden had started to melt snow with a view to carrying hot fluid back up the mountain for Ian. This proved to be unnecessary as Ian was able to make his own wobbly way back to Camp 3. On arrival he looked terrible. He could barely stand. His eyes were bloodshot and he couldn't speak.

We piled him into the tent and plied him with hot fluid and a high flow of oxygen. When he could he said that his feet were cold and that he hadn't felt his toes for some time. We decided to leave his boots on because if frost bitten we wouldn't be able to get them back on again and descent would be even trickier."

At 1pm he had recovered a little and he and Pasang set off down again and made it to the North Col where they met up with Mick and Matt. They all descended to ABC.

Once again, I recorded:

"An amazing job by Ian, Pasang and the rest of the team to get from near death at the bottom of the Second Step all the way down to the North Col and ABC. Ian is in a terrible state. He is blind in his right eye. His speech is slurred and he can hardly balance. He has minor frost bite in one toe. He was understandably very emotional about six dead bodies he saw up there and what he called the emptiness of the summit experience. Except for the view, he said, it was no holy grail."

Dr John shared his tent with him that night and Ian slept on oxygen - a fantastic team effort.

Apparently, a member of the Indian Air Force Team died above Camp 3 the same day. It is possible that they lacked both some of the tangible resources that we had in terms of personal altitude kits, oxygen supplies and hot drinks and the intangible and powerful bond of friends working together to help each other. We had all tried our best to prepare ourselves for the climb and unlike on most other mountains we had a safe line of descent down the fixed ropes from Camp 3. Perhaps something similar had happened to Pete Boardman and Joe Tasker but they had nowhere to go?

Back in the UK Ian made a full recovery and a few years later climbed Ama Dablam. He is now a rope access worker.

Tim runs a successful climbing/guiding and instruction business in the UK and Nepal under his own name of Tim Mosedale.

Stuart is a full-time photographer, adventurer and paraglider. Check out his video of jumping from the summit of Ama Dablam.

Mick married his girlfriend, became a father and now lives on Vancouver Island where he runs a worldwide trekking business called Wilderness Trekking.

Matt left KE and is also now a husband and father and works in the film industry.

Dan alternates between doing rope access work and being front of house at the KE offices in Keswick.

Ross recovered from his DVT and continues running his outdoor business in North Wales.

Karma, Jangbu and Phanden have been back to Everest and Phanden has led two expeditions to Shishapangma, the only 8000m peak entirely in Tibet. Between times they continue to work with KE groups in Nepal. Phanden has visited the UK several times and has set up his own business called Sherpa Climbing.

Pasang spent some time in the UK before returning to Nepal to set up his own trekking agency.

On Everest we had all tried our hardest, worked together and had just got away with it. We had finished up just on the right side of the line. The late Alex Lowe once said that the best climber is the one who has the most fun. By that criterion we were also undoubtedly the best team on the mountain.

Postscript

Early in 2011 I was with my friend Don Gladstone at Plas Y Brenin for a meeting. In the evening I gave a slide show and lecture to the students about the Himalaya. As is traditional at the end I asked if there were any questions. Two young climbers at the front who had been studying every picture and listening to my every word put their hands up.

The first said:

"You have done loads of trips, how do you get the sponsorship?"

I said :

"I don't. I do it the old fashioned way. I either go to work and save up or it *is* my work and I get paid."

The second one then asked:

"What is your greatest mountaineering achievement?"

"That's easy," I replied, "reaching 56 years of age."

Epilogue

In 2008, on my way up towards the Zatrwa La from the airstrip at Lukla en route yet again to Mera Peak with a KE group, I bumped into someone I hadn't seen for years. It was Ray Delaney, Joe Simpson's friend and climbing partner on our Pumo Ri trip in 1995.

He and another friend had been exploring the possibility of climbing a new route on the South Face of Mera. The route taken by all groups on Mera goes round to the other side from the Mera La to the north. The normal ascent route, although high and cold, is basically roped-up walking. The South Face in contrast is huge, complex, objectively dangerous and very steep. Up until that time there was only one route that had been climbed on it. That was by the late Mal Duff and the late "Tat" Tattersall, both friends of Joe's and Ray's.

Ray and his friend had trekked to the bottom of the face in poor weather and had been intimidated by the likely difficulty and danger it presented. They had done a bit of reconnaissance but no climbing. In early 2009 Ray asked Joe to join him to try to climb a new route on the Face. Joe emailed me asking if I had any good pictures of it. I had and it looked scary.

In October Joe and Ray went to Nepal to give it a try. Joe had done little serious climbing for years but was nonetheless driven by the notion that people judged him badly as a climber. In fact he had always been a talented climber as well as a great survivor. In pursuit of proving himself he had also tried several times to climb the North Face of the Eiger in Switzerland but had been driven back by weather and back luck. Over the years, Joe and I had drifted apart a bit. We had fallen out over the Pumo Ri trip in 1995, but that was a long time ago and somehow, with our busy lives, we had never quite got round to having a few beers together or anything. Making up was not something we would do. If asked we probably would both describe each other as a mate, but we hadn't seen each other for ages.

Ray rang me at my hotel and we did have a few beers in Kathmandu before my group arrived and before they left to attempt their new route. I really hoped that they would go and have a look and, like the previous year, then give up and go home. It seems like a dangerous place for anyone, let alone two people approaching middle age who hadn't climbed anything like it for years. Ray had a family and business commitments and Joe had fairly recently begun what sounded like an important relationship with Corinne.

As was so often the case before, Joe proved me wrong. On the 31st October I was having a doze in my tent at the High Camp on Mera at about 5800m. It is a magnificent location. The tents are secured on a series of ledges above a huge drop down to the Neulekh Glacier with views stretching to Chamlang, Baruntse and Makalu and, in the far distance, Kangchenjunga. I was woken from my slumbers by a voice near my tent. It was Joe asking a Sherpa if I was in the camp. I quickly came to and got out expecting to warmly greet Joe and Ray having much to my surprise climbed their new route. Joe was however alone. I was confused and initially panicked. Was Ray dead? I felt sick. It took a few minutes of explanation to clarify things.

Ray had decided that the only possible route was too objectively dangerous and had decided not to climb. Joe felt differently and set off alone and over three days he climbed it. He collapsed in my tent and over the next couple of days ate, slept and trekked with us as we came down from our summit next morning.

He, I think, had felt that he had proven something to himself or to some notional body of critics that he was a competent climber. Afterwards he declared that he had given up climbing and sold or gave away his gear. I am certain that he has. It was as if a burden had been lifted.

Afterwards Joe and Ray went off to holiday in Nepal. Joe gave me a letter to give to Corinne. He had already spoken to her on the phone, so the contents would not have been quite so shocking to read. It was, as I understood it from Joe, the "If when you read this I am dead" letter. Joe was never very good at talking about emotions, but I would guess as ever great at writing about them.

We still go to the pub from time to time and as always argue endlessly about most things.

Mountains of course in themselves have no intrinsic meaning; they are just rock and ice. It is all about the interpretation and values that we put on them and there are as many different ones of those as there are mountains. There is also no mantra, spell or potion that can guarantee that you won't get killed by them either.

Mountaineering Chronology

International Mountaineering Experience:

Expeditions to 8000m Peaks are underlined.

1976 Swiss Alps Saas Fe
1977 Mount Kenya
1978 Swiss Alps Arolla and ISM (International School of
         Mountaineering) Alpine Mountaineering Course.
1979 Kulu Himalaya India. Brent Himalayan Expedition
1980 French Alps, Dauphine/Ecrin area.
1981 Mount Kenya.
1982 French Alps Chamonix and Zermatt
1984 Chamonix
1985 Tent Peak (Tharpu Chuli), Nepal
1986 Chamonix
1987 Tupopdan Expedition, Karakoram, Pakistan
1988 Hushe Karakoram, Pakistan; Rupina La Trek Nepal
1989 Toupopdan again
1990 Snow Lake, Pakistan
1991 Pumo Ri, Nepal
1992 Rupina La Trek, Nepal
1993 Khumbu Trek and Island Peak (Imja Tse), Nepal
1994 Khumbu Trek
1995 Lobuche Peak Nepal; Elbrus, Bezingi Area, Gumachi,
         Caucasus, Russia; Hindu Kush, Pakistan; Tent Peak
         Nepal
1996 Langtang Trek; Chulu Far West Annapurna Area,
         Tent Peak and Pumo Ri; Mera and Island Peak, Nepal
1997 Khumbu trek, Rolwaling; Mera Peak, Nepal
1998 Khumbu trek, Nepal; _Cho Oyu Expedition, Tibet_;
         Markha Valley Trek, Ladakh, India; _Cho Oyu_
         Expedition, Tibet; Mera Peak, Nepal; Annapurna
         Circuit, Nepal
1999 Mount Aspiring, New Zealand; _Cho Oyu_

Expedition,Tibet; Naya Kanga, Nepal; Tent Peak,
Nepal; Mera and Island Peak, Nepal

2000 Illamani, Huayno Potosi and Peguano, Alpamayo,
Bolivia; Cho Oyu Expedition, Tibet; Tent Peak, Nepal;
Cotopaxi (2), Cayambe and Chimborazo, Ecuador

2001 Kilimanjaro, Tanzania; Gasherbrum 2, Karakoram,
Pakistan; Khumbu trek; Nepal; Mera and Island Peak,
Nepal

2002 Mera Peak, Nepal

2003 Lhotse, Nepal; Khumbu Trek Nepal; Lhakpa Ri
(7045m) Tibet

2004 Mera Peak, Nepal; Singalila Ridge and Goecha La
Trek, Sikkim, India; Mount Khuiten and Narindal, Altai
Tavan Bogd Trek, Kharkhiraa Valley, Mongolia; Lhakpa
Ri, Tibet; Lobuche, Island and Parchamo Peaks,
Nepal.

2005 Ruwenzori Mountains, Stanley and Speke, Uganda;
Karrimor Everest North Ridge Expedition; Gondoro La
Trek, Karakoram, Pakistan; Mera Peak and Yala Peak,
Nepal

2006 Winter High Atlas Mountains, Morocco; Mera and
Lobuche, Pokalde and Island Peaks Nepal; Mount
Khuiten and Narindal, Altai Tavan Bogd, Mongolia;
Lhakpa Ri, Tibet

2007 Winter High Atlas Mountains Morocco, Lobuche, Island
Peaks Nepal

2008 Winter High Atlas Mountains, Morocco; Mera Peak,
Nepal; Mount Khuiten and Narindal, Altai Tavan Bogd
Mongolia; Gangotri Area, India; Snowman Trek,
Bhutan; Mera Peak, Nepal; Lhakpa Ri, Tibet

2009 Winter High Atlas Mountains, Morocco; Peak Lenin,
Kyrgyzstan; Mera Peak (2), Nepal

2010 Winter High Atlas Mountains Morocco (3); Mera Peak,
Nepal; Everest Kangshung Face trek, Tibet; Mount
Khuiten and Narindal, Altai Tavan Bogd, Mongolia;
Cradle Mountain, Tasmania, Australia; Simeon

Mountains, Ethiopia (2)
2011 Winter High Atlas Mountains, Morocco; Everest Trek,
Tent Peak, Nepal; Stok Kangri and Markha Valley,
Ladakh India

Gear Editor for CLIMB magazine from 2006 – present.
Ambassador for TEKO for Nepal from 2008 – present
Ambassador for Rab from 2007– 2011
Ambassador for Karrimor 1999 - 2007

Glossary of Mountaineering Terms and other Information

Abseil A rapid method of descent involving sliding down a rope. The speed of descent is controlled by an abseil device.

Abseil Device A metal instrument usually in a figure of eight shape that attaches a climber to an abseil rope.

Aconcagua (6960m) The highest mountain in South America.

Acclimatisation The adaptation by the human body to the rarefied air at altitude. If ascent is too fast above approximately 2500m acute mountain sickness (AMS) can be experienced and if left untreated can lead to the life-threatening High Altitude Cerebral Oedema (HACE) and High Altitude Pulmonary Oedema (HAPE).

Alpine Style A technique of climbing that involves a small party moving simultaneously roped together over rock, snow and ice terrain without resort to pre-fixed ropes and camps. Considered to be a purer style of ascent.

Alpine Club The first climbing club in the world, founded in 1857.

Bhai The affectionate and respectful Nepali term literally meaning younger brother but also used to close younger friends.

Belay The technique of safeguarding a climber in the event of a fall. Used to both refer to the paying-out of the rope to another climber and the method of securing oneself to the mountain.

Boardman, Pete Was on Chris Bonington's Everest Expedition of 1975 and made the third British ascent of the mountain and the first alpine style ascent of Kangchenjunga. Pete died attempting a first, alpine style, without bottled oxygen, ascent of the North-East ridge of Everest.

Burn A Scottish term used to refer to streams and small rivers.

Chimborazo (6267m) The highest peak in Ecuador.

Col A mountain pass or saddle. The lowest point between two adjoining peaks.

Coire A term used in Scotland to describe a glacial bowl, referred to elsewhere as a cwm or cirque.

Cornice An overhanging edge of snow formed along a ridge by wind.

Cotopaxi (5897m) A popular snow-capped volcano in the Cordillera Oriental in Ecuador.

Couloir A French word for a gully.

Crampons A framework of metal spikes attached to the bottom of mountaineering boots for movement on snow and ice.

Crevasse A crack in the surface of a glacier. Size and shape can vary greatly. Climbers generally move roped together on glaciers in order to aid rescue if someone falls in one. Snow cover can make crevasses very difficult to see.

Dhai The affectionate and respectful Nepali term literally meaning older brother but also used for close older friends.

Fixed Ropes   Series of ropes previously attached to the mountain or rockface by climbers to enable safe ascent and descent for groups or for setting up camps above. Ascent is usually made with a <u>Jumar.</u>

Frostbite   The freezing of the body's extremities. It is caused by extreme cold and wind and exacerbated by poor equipment, dehydration and exhaustion. There are different degrees of frostbite, the earliest of which can heal if treated correctly.

Gaiters   Knee-high tubes of waterproof material that prevent snow and rocks from entering the tops of boots. Usually open with a front zip and some extend to cover the upper of the boots.

Glacier   In effect a river of ice forming in high mountains. They are generally retreating since the last ice age. They still can be up to a 1km thick.

Gendarme   An isolated pinnacle of rock on a mountain.

Habeler, Peter   A highly accomplished Austrian Mountain Guide who became most famous for making the first ascent of Everest without bottled oxygen with Reinhold Messner.

Haston, Dougal   A famous Scottish climber who amongst many things made the first ascent of the South Face of Annapurna and the first British ascent of Everest. He died in a skiing accident in 1977.

Icefall   Sections of some glaciers that flow downhill steeply, where crevasses form and blocks break off due to the movement.

Jumar   A handled device that locks on a rope in the event of a downward pull but which can be freely slid up it. Used for ascending fixed ropes.

K2 (8611m)   The second highest mountain in the world. It is situated in the Pakistan/Chinese Karakoram.

Kangchenjunga (8586m)   The third highest mountain in the world. It is located on the India/Nepal border.

Karabiner   A metal snaplink used in belaying, abseiling and many other purposes in climbing.

Khuiten, Mount (4374m)   The highest mountain in Mongolia.

Kilimanjaro (5895m)   A walk-up peak on the Tanzania/Kenya Border. It is the highest mountain in Africa.

Messner, Reinhold   Arguably the greatest mountaineer in history. He was the first to climb all the 8000m+ mountains of the world and Everest without bottled oxygen.

Moraine   Unconsolidated heaps of rubble created by the advancing and retreating action of a glacier.

Munro   The term given to any mountain in Scotland over 3000 ft in height.

Névé   A French term for relatively new snow that has been repeatedly frozen and thawed but not enough to become ice.

Rockfall   A quantity of rock that falls freely down a cliff or mountain.

Rouse, Alan   One of the most accomplished British climbers of the 70s and 80s. He died after reaching the summit making the first British ascent of K2.

Solo climbing Climbing alone either with or without the use of a rope.

White-out A condition where falling snow, cloud and the snow underfoot become indistinguishable, making orientation and navigation very difficult and dangerous.

Acknowledgements

This book started as therapy for me and turned into a story, the lessons from which I hadn't allowed into my consciousness, let alone got the measure of until I began the process of writing. I have arrived not at a conclusion but more of an understanding with no clear simple answer.

It has been an enjoyable and demanding task and one in which I have aimed to celebrate the fun, the friendships and the high adventure and at the same time acknowledge the huge price that sometimes is paid for it.

I couldn't have written more than a page or so without the help of many people in many different ways.

Firstly thanks must go to Janet James for her love, patience, support and confidence in me and my ability.

To Don Gladstone for his ideas and criticisms and for not quite falling asleep when I read samples to him. To Barry Fletcher, my long time friend and more recently publisher for being both. To Rosie Smith for editing my repetitious ramblings with skill and tact. To Emily Roberts for her creativity and patience over the cover design. To Andy Cave another long-time friend and one time lodger for writing the Foreword. To Dave Pickford my Editor at Climb magazine for his thoughts and ideas. To Stuart Holmes, Rod Pawsey and Greenshires Publishing for permission to use some of their pictures. To Mike Pedler and Liz Tye at the Hope Valley Literary Festival for their invitation.

To my friend from Primary school Steve Williams for help with scanning my dusty old 35mm slides.

Also indirectly several other people and organisations have helped by enabling me to live the life I have. They include Andy Broom, for taking me on in the first place, all at KE Adventure Travel and Dick Turnbull, Fran Beardon, Rob Turnbull and Jez Portman at Outside Ltd for being exceptionally tolerant employers. Thank you.